GO NATIVE

Your guide to growing native Hawaiian and canoe plants wherever you live, work or play

by
Hilary Parkinson
Paul Arinaga
Jonathan Price
Tom Foye

An initiative of the Hawai'i Forest Institute

Illustrations by Kim Sielbeck Ltd.
Graphic Design by Susan Anderegg

The information in this book is true and complete to the best of our knowledge. All recommendations are made without guarantee on the part of the authors or the Hawai'i Forest Institute (HFI). The authors and publisher disclaim any liability in connection with the use of this information.

The mission of the Hawai'i Forest Institute is to promote the health and productivity of Hawaii's forests through forest restoration, educational programs, information dissemination, and support for scientific research.

Publisher:
The Hawai'i Forest Institute
P.O. Box 66
O'okala HI 96774
Phone: 808-933-9411

HFI website: www.hawaiiforestinstitute.org

Go Native website: www.gonativeplants.org

This book is dedicated to all
the native Hawaiian plants that managed to reach—by wave,
wind, or wing—the most isolated island chain in the world and thrive.
And to the Polynesian-introduced canoe plants that provided life and sustenance
to the Hawaiian people. May native Hawaiian plants thrive once again,
and canoe plants continue to sustain us all.

Table of Contents

Acknowledgements

Aubry Kae Andersen, graphic designer, stepped in to help us revise and improve Chapter One and skillfully complete the graphic design work. Throughout the process she quickly addressed challenges creatively and proficiently. We are extremely grateful for her generously donating 50% of her time to this work.

Orville Baldos, assistant professor/researcher in ornamental horticulture at the University of Hawaiʻi at Mānoa (UHM), kindly met with us on multiple occasions to provide feedback on plant selection for designs and answer numerous questions on species he's researched.

Rick Barboza, native plant specialist and owner of Hui Kū Maoli Ola Nursery, generously offered his time to review the Quick Reference Table and gave encouragement for this work when it was first being developed. Nurseries like his are what makes a publication like this possible. He has sustainably collected and grown the vast majority of plants featured in this guide, making them available at his nursery in Kaneohe as well as retail outlets like City Mill and Home Depot. He knows native plants like few others, having traveled the islands far and wide to observe them in their natural environment AND observe how they respond in built environments. We can offer plants appropriate to your zone, and suggest some designs, but Rick Barboza can make suggestions on subspecies or species alternatives based on conditions unique to your site. When planning your landscape, if you're able to hire someone like Rick Barboza with decades of experience with native plants, we strongly encourage you to do so to complement the material provided here.

Franny Brewer, Big Island Invasive Species Council, provided helpful feedback on plants to include in the Quick Reference Table and designs, and assisted with the development of the Nursery List.

David Eickhoff, native plant specialist, generously offered his time to review the Quick Reference Table and provided feedback on plant selections for some of the designs. The Quick Reference Table would not have been possible without the information compiled by him and others in the http://nativeplants.hawaii.edu/ website. We are also grateful for his incredible photos (https://www.flickr.com/photos/dweickhoff/).

J.B. Friday, Extension Forester, College of Tropical Agriculture and Human Resources, UH Mānoa, proofed the first draft of the Quick Reference Table, kindly answered many questions (and more questions), created a special photo album for us to use, provided a critical addition to the "FAQ and More Resources" section regarding Rapid ʻŌhiʻa Death, and helped connect us to numerous people and resources.

Sam ʻOhukaniʻōhiʻa Gon III, conservation biologist and Hawaiian cultural practitioner, offered feedback on zones and mapping when the project was first developing and connected us to co-author J.P. Price. We are grateful for his forward arising from his deep roots in both the ecological and cultural realms.

Butch Haase, Executive Director at Molokai Land Trust, generously offered his time to review plant selections and landscape designs. His background in landscaping, as well as restoration ecology made his comments and feedback incredibly helpful.

Travis Idol, Associate Professor of Tropical Forestry and Agroforestry, UH Mānoa, and President of the Hawaiʻi Forest Institute, co-created the original concept for the Go Native Project, provided feedback during the early development of this guide and reviewed content.

Kerin E Lilleng-Rosenberger, native plant specialist and author of *Growing Hawaii's Native Plants: A Simple Step-by-step Approach for Every Species*, shared her feedback on the scope and intent of this guide and reinforced the need, brought up by co-author Tom Foye, for a "Community Portal" as a complement to this guide to help troubleshoot problems once plants are in the ground.

Noa Lincoln, Assistant Professor, Indigenous Crops and Cropping Systems, Department of Tropical Plants and Soil Sciences, UH Mānoa, provided feedback on zones and information on the canoe plants in the Quick Reference Table.

Heather McMillen, Hawaiʻi State Urban Forester, Kaulunani Program Coordinator, provided the founding funds to make the Go Native Project possible and enabled us to collaborate with other Kaulunani grantees at a workshop and via introductions. We are grateful for the urban forestry perspective expressed in her foreword.

Jesse Mikasobe-Kealiinohomoku, Mālama Learning Center, provided a tour of the native Hawaiian and canoe plant garden at the Mālama Learning Center site in Kunia, answered numerous questions about species combinations, and had recommendations for the "FAQ and More Resources" section regarding growing kalo.

Molly Murphy, Big Island Invasive Species Council, provided helpful feedback on plants to include in the Quick Reference Table as well as designs, and assisted with the development of the Nursery List.

Elliott Parsons, Forest Reserve Manager, Natural Area Reserves Specialist IV, Division of Forestry and Wildlife, UH Hilo, provided feedback on species combinations for zones. We appreciated his suggestion to add information on FireWise Landscaping to the "FAQs and More Resources" section.

Richard Quinn, Landscape Architect, gave us an informative tour of the native plant garden he designed and manages at the Shidler School of Business at UH Mānoa and provided feedback on plant selection and designs. He has fielded numerous questions over the last year and we have so appreciated his support and encouragement.

Pauline Sato, Executive Director and Co-Founder of the Mālama Learning Center, offered valuable feedback on plant combinations for designs and kindly offered us a booth to promote this project at the Mālama Learning Center Arbor Day event.

Heather Simmons, Executive Director of the Hawai'i Forest Institute, reviewed drafts and in her role as executive director has encouraged this effort since it's inception.

Forest and Kim Starr, Biologists and Environmental Consultants, provide an incredible public resource in their collection of plant photos (http://www.starrenvironmental.com/), and half of the photos in Chapter 4 are theirs.

Aileen Yeh, owner of Aileen's nursery, reviewed plant selections for some designs and provided feedback on species availability in the nursery trade.

Funders

This project was made possible by the support of the **Kaulunani Urban and Community Forestry Program** of the DLNR Division of Forestry and Wildlife, and State and Private Forestry, branch of the U.S. Forest Service, Region 5.

The Hawai'i Forest Institute would also like to thank **The Atherton Family Foundation**, **The Steve and Gloria Gainsley Fund of the Hawai'i Community Foundation**, and **The Kosasa Foundation** for their generous support.

In accordance with Federal civil rights law and U.S. Department of Agriculture (USDA) civil rights regulations and policies, the USDA, its Agencies, offices, and employees, and institutions participating in or administering USDA programs are prohibited from discriminating based on race, color, national origin, religion, sex, gender identity (including gender expression), sexual orientation, disability, age, marital status, family/parental status, income derived from a public assistance program, political beliefs, or reprisal or retaliation for prior civil rights activity, in any program or activity conducted or funded by USDA (not all bases apply to all programs). Remedies and complaint filing deadlines vary by program or incident.

Forewords

Before contact with the Western World, Hawai'i was home to not only a rich ecological setting that generated thousands of plants and animals found nowhere else on Earth, but that same unique and rich living environment enabled Hawaiians to create a pinnacle of Polynesian civilizations. It was one built not only of the plants and animals they had brought from Tahiti, but on the many endemic plants that provided for tools, shelter, medicines, foods and other material trappings, and which lent stable resilient ecosystems and watersheds that were recognized as the foundation of life. Those native wild places were granted godly status as the *wao akua*—the realm of the gods.

Thus, the many native Hawaiian plants were revered, not only the majestic koa and 'ōhi'a trees towering overhead, but even the smallest native ferns of the forest floor, that, belying their stature were the *kinolau*—physical manifestation—of the major gods. Hawaiians knew the names of their rich flora, and the character of plants shaped the intellectual and spiritual foundations of Hawaiian life. Places were celebrated via their signature plants—the delicate lehua 'āhihi of wet Nu'uanu, or the gnarled wiliwili groves of ghost-filled 'Ewa. Even in the most heavily cultivated areas, native plants were immediate neighbors to cultivated ones, in semi-wild systems that maintained ecological processes to the benefit of both people and native species. Indeed, the most important cordage plant cultivated, olonā, was an endemic Hawaiian species whose stem fibers are still recognized as the strongest plant-based fibers on Earth.

So much was lost when large-scale Western agriculture, be it sugar, pineapple, or ranches, erased the thousands of native plants from the lowlands of Hawai'i. People largely lost their physical, intellectual, and spiritual connections with the native plants that once defined them, and Hawai'i soldiers in WWII were called "pineapples" in a dim echo of how native plants had once defined them. Hawaiian culture along with Hawaiian species were pushed to the brink of extinction…

But we live in exciting times now where there is a renaissance of culture, and a growing recognition of the value of native plants, of places that still hold their native character, and of efforts to return the natives to the landscape. What you are reading here is an expression of that movement, and an opportunity to take an active role in bringing native nature back to developed places. In doing so we rebuild that which defines Hawai'i as a unique place on Earth, and reforge our connection to our islands. Go Native!

Dr. Sam 'Ohukani'ōhi'a Gon III
Conservation Biologist and Hawaiian Cultural Practitioner

Around the world, the vegetation that is interwoven throughout towns and cities locates people in a particular space and time, and it provides a sense of place. In Hawai'i, we are witnessing a growing movement to reclaim our communities and be intentional about place-making by creating cultural landscapes that root us to the history and genealogies of the 'āina. These stories are anchored by the first to inhabit our islands, our beloved native plants and also by the landscapes that the Polynesians who first voyaged to Hawai'i transported in their canoes. Today, the chance to not just visit, but intimately know and build relationships with native Hawaiian plants should not be reserved for the relative few who are able to access protected and remote areas where remnant native forest remains. Similarly, knowing and building relationships with Polynesian-introduced plants could be common here in Hawai'i. Everyone should have the opportunity to live among, touch, smell, taste, care for, and use native Hawaiian and Polynesian-introduced plants in their daily lives. This guide helps to facilitate those relationships through sharing which plants are best for which places, and encouraging us to create, re-create, and innovate new spaces around our homes that resonate with the continuity of Hawai'i's ancient relationships between people and plants. I encourage you to not just learn *about* the plants in the guide, but to take the next steps. Go Native! Involve your family in planting and caring for these beloved plants so that you may learn *from* them and create new stories together as an extended family. *I ola 'oe, i ola mākou nei.* When they thrive, we thrive!

Dr. Heather McMillen
Urban & Community Forester, Hawai'i Division of Forestry and Wildlife

Chapter One

This guide is designed to help you grow native Hawaiian and Polynesian-introduced ("canoe") plants in your landscaping. The guide is intended for a broad audience including novice gardeners, experienced gardeners, landscape architects, business owners, school teachers and administrators, recreational park managers, horticulturists, and conservationists—basically, anyone who might be interested in growing native Hawaiian and canoe plants.

Introduction

To support your success in growing native Hawaiian and canoe plants, we've presented combinations of plants that do well together in your specific growing zone. We've also tried to account for differences in personal tastes, growing space available, and amount of gardening experience. Our aim is to provide easy to follow "recipes", while enabling people to substitute some ingredients (plants) in case they want more or less of a particular "taste". On the design spectrum from the formal (plants evenly spaced, symmetrical, and following a geometric pattern) to the informal (more curving lines, spaced as plants would exist naturally), we are on the latter end of the spectrum. However, you can arrange the components as you wish for the garden design you want; our goal is to provide you with the tools and inspiration to do so. We have highlighted three landscaping scenarios for each of the eight growing zones. Even if you don't use these "as is" we hope that they will inspire you to create designs that fit your space and needs.

This guide follows in the footsteps of a long line of excellent books about native Hawaiian plants, many of which are referenced in the included resource guide. There are numerous books with details on how to grow specific plants or about the plants themselves, and we recommend that you consult them. The Go Native guide attempts to do something different: our aim is to provide you with easy-to-follow designs and combinations of plants that are suitable to your growing zone.

The Go Native Project

This guide is a key part of the Go Native: Growing a Native Hawaiian Urban Forest project. The goal of the Go Native project is to encourage Hawaii's residents, businesses, and other organizations to grow more native Hawaiian and canoe plants. We also hope to increase public awareness of the value and benefits of planting native plants and trees. Our goal, which you can read more about below, is to mobilize the public to create a series of kīpuka or micro-forests within the urban and suburban core. These garden patches of native Hawaiian and canoe plants can form a Native Hawaiian Urban Forest that can connect with natural forests.

How we suggest you use the guide:

1. **Use the growing zone maps to figure out the growing zone in which you'll be planting.** An approximation is fine; this is not an exact science. If you find yourself seemingly on the border between two zones, perhaps you can explore both zones. Some experimentation may be required. This becomes even more necessary when human intervention has altered natural characteristics. For example, drainage installed on your site may change natural moisture levels.

2. **Decide which of the three landscaping scenarios best fits your needs.** Depending on your situation and personal tastes, you may use it "as is", incorporate it into a larger landscaping plan, or use bits and pieces of it.

3. **Refer to the recommended assemblage of plants for your growing zone and scenario.** You can (and probably should) also look them up in the quick reference table.

4. **Use the quick reference table to find other plants** to complement or replace the ones in the suggested scenario, depending upon your needs or personal tastes.

Conservation and YOU: A Call to Action!

During both world wars, because of drastic food shortages in the U.S. and abroad, Americans were encouraged to start Victory Gardens in their yards to grow fruits and vegetables. Even those without yards were able to participate by growing in window boxes or on rooftops. At its peak during World War II, the U.S. Dept. of Agriculture estimates that there were about 20 million Victory Gardens across the U.S., and by 1944, Victory Gardens were responsible for growing approximately 40% of all the fruits and vegetables in the country. In Hawai'i during WWII, there were 20,000 Victory Gardens, or one for every 21 people.

While we encourage you to volunteer at conservation sites across these islands, we also hope that this book will inspire you to plant native Hawaiian plants in your own yard, or whatever space you may have available. This is something that *everyone* can do. As you can see in the accompanying chart, over 10% of endemic species are now extinct and introduced plants out number native plants by more than six times.

As with the Victory Gardens of the past, by working together we can once again realize similar results, but this time for native Hawaiian plants. If everyone pitches in and uses whatever growing space they have—no matter how small—within one generation or less we can realize the Native Hawaiian Urban Forest Network. ***Go Native!***

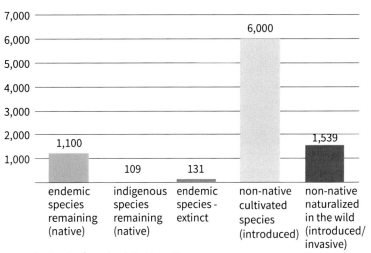

Native Hawaiian Plants face an onslaught

endemic species remaining (native)	1,100
indigenous species remaining (native)	109
endemic species - extinct	131
non-native cultivated species (introduced)	6,000
non-native naturalized in the wild (introduced/invasive)	1,539

Endemic: found only in Hawai'i
Indigenous: native to Hawai'i and other places
Source: Dr. Tim Gallaher, Botanist for the Bernice Pauahi Bishop Museum

*For more information and to join the **Go Native** movement, please visit **www.gonativeplants.org***

How it All Started

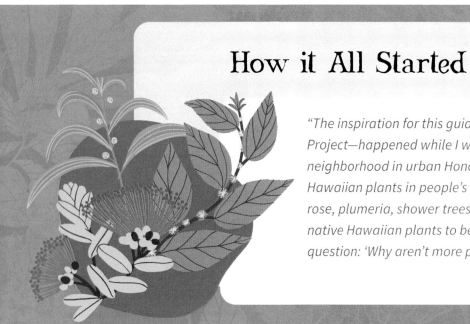

"The inspiration for this guide—and, indeed, for the entire Go Native Project—happened while I was taking a leisurely stroll around my neighborhood in urban Honolulu. I was struck by the lack of native Hawaiian plants in people's landscaping. There were plenty of desert rose, plumeria, shower trees, and, of course, lawns, but very few native Hawaiian plants to be seen anywhere. This prompted a simple question: 'Why aren't more people growing native Hawaiian plants?'"

– Paul Arinaga

Is it hard to grow native Hawaiian plants?

The answer, we would discover, was more complex than originally thought. In the first place, we found out that many people have a misconception that growing native Hawaiian plants is hard. Perhaps this is because so many native Hawaiian plants have gone extinct or are endangered (1 out of 10 native Hawaiian plant species are already extinct). After all, if native Hawaiian plants can't survive then they must be hard to grow, right? Experimenting with plants such as the modest, yet miraculous pōhinahina (left), we discovered that while some native Hawaiian plants may be difficult to grow, others are not.

"Right Plant, Right Place"

In speaking with members of the community and through our own growing successes and failures, we also discovered that many failures are the result of trying to grow a plant in a place that is simply not suited to it. The huge diversity in climate zones in Hawai'i, which has 10 of the world's 14 zones, makes this challenging. This led to a key realization and the core principle of this guide: to increase one's success in growing native Hawaiian plants, it's essential to identify the optimal growing zone in which they can thrive. "Right plant, right place" is a core tenet of the Kaulunani Urban and Community Forestry Program of the DLNR Division of Forestry and Wildlife (which provided the seed funding for this project). This realization in turn led us to Dr. Jonathan Price, a professor of Tropical Conservation Biology and Environmental Science at UH Hilo who, along with Dr. Sam Gon (see his foreword) and others, has conducted research to map the natural geographic ranges of plant species in the Hawaiian Islands based on

> "To increase one's success in growing native Hawaiian plants, it's essential to identify the optimal growing zone in which they can thrive."

factors such as moisture level (factoring in precipitation and temperature), elevation, topography, soil type, and substrate age. We adapted the research by Dr. Price and his colleagues to develop eight growing zones for this book. For each of these eight growing zones, we've listed combinations of plants that grow well in the zone. The hope is to increase your growing success rate by offering suggested combinations of plants that are perfectly suited to your location and work well together.

How are native Hawaiian plants different?

While growing native Hawaiian plants is not always hard, it is different. By visiting several native Hawaiian gardens and interviewing experts, we gradually realized that growing native Hawaiian plants is not the same as growing non-native landscaping plants. Most plants sold for landscaping have been bred and selected to reliably produce certain traits such as consistent growth form and size, flower, or leaf color, and in some cases pest or disease resistance. While there's certainly variation among species, these plants are typically "obedient". In contrast, most (but not all) native Hawaiian plants are not. They evolved over 3-5 million years on the most isolated island chain in the world without human contact. Only in the last 1,000 years have humans been involved.

Makani, Moana, Manu: By Wind, Wave, and Wing

Once every 100,000 years, a new plant made landfall by chance and established itself in the isolated Hawaiian Islands. Pōhuehue (middle right) and naupaka (top right) are examples of plants that arrived by water with seeds that float and are unaffected by salt water. Ferns like hāpu'u (bottom right) with tiny spores arrived by wind. Plants having sticky fruits such as the pa-pala kepau may have been brought on the plumage of birds blown to Hawai'i by storms, while plants with indigest-ible seeds like the akala or Hawaiian raspberry could have been carried within the digestive tracts of birds.

FOREST & KIM STARR

DAVID EICKHOFF

A new landscaping aesthetic: has its time come?

What does all this mean for the landscape architect or homeowner who wants to start growing native Hawaiian plants in their landscaping? We believe that it may be time to consider an alternative landscaping aesthetic. The current aesthetic is, for the most part, static and controlled. Homeowners and businesses may pay a landscape architect to design and install "instant" landscaping that rarely or never changes. An urban landscape should also be well-manicured; plants need to behave. If they don't, they may be trimmed or replaced. Lastly, typical urban landscaping is clearly a human creation.

There is nothing inherently wrong with this aesthetic. Without it, we would not have many of the horticultural wonders of the world such as the gardens at Versailles in France, Kew near London, Keukenhof in the Netherlands, the Butchart Gardens in Victoria, British Columbia, or perhaps even the rock garden at Ryōanji. Traditional landscaping aesthetics are, however, often very different from how native plants grow in the wild. Ecological succession, or one plant replacing another over time, is a natural phenomenon in a native ecosystem. A plant finds a niche—a spot with the sunlight, moisture, and nutrients it needs—but through time, it may be replaced by a larger or more competitive species. Conditions change and plant communities respond, thus making ecosystems dynamic, not static.

The native Hawaiian garden at the Shidler College of Business, UH Mānoa. Design by Rick Quinn.

Even native Hawaiian urban gardens, such as the one planted and managed by local landscape architect Rick Quinn near the Shidler College of Business on the University of Hawai'i at Mānoa campus, have changed over time. Rick's garden has developed as conditions in it such as tree shade and the soil composition have changed; some plants have flourished while others have died off. The person planting a native Hawaiian garden may need to be more open to change and to letting a degree of ecological succession play out. In this sense, gardening becomes a journey of experimentation and discovery rather than a one-time installation.

Rewilding?

In *Planting in a Post Wild World*, authors Thomas Rainier and Claudia West write that people are starting to see nature not as something only on far away mountaintops. It can also exist in built environments like suburban yards, utility easements, rooftops, and right of ways. They urge that we start to see urban places with fresh eyes to cut "through the layers of concrete and asphalt to see new hybrids of natural and man-made, of horticulture and ecology." While we can't expect to recreate the diverse communities of intact forests in urban yards, we can nonetheless make a small shift. We would humbly like to suggest that perhaps some form of "rewilding"—or restoring an area to its natural uncultivated state—can find a place in your garden, too.

Users of this book do not need to let their gardens become "jungles", however. We have seen examples of flourishing urban gardens that use native Hawaiian plants yet are well-manicured and do not change greatly over time (see the picture to the right of the Diamond Head residence designed by Rick Quinn). Moreover, we recognize that the human eye needs something that looks coherent and intentional. Surprisingly, an intact native ecosystem can be just that. On the north shore of O'ahu, for example, there are large groups of naupaka kahakai *(Scaevola taccada)*, borders of hinahina *(Heliotropium anomalum)*, and pockets of 'ohai *(Sesbania tomentosa)*. It is possible to recreate this beauty in designed plant communities, and as the authors of *Planting in a Post Wild World* note: "the solution lies in understanding plantings as a community of compatible species that cover the ground in interlocking layers."

Our design section suggests how to form these layers be it on your lanai, a walkway outside your business, or in your yard. Co-author Hilary Parkinson has been careful to select combinations of plants—vetted by numerous experts in the field—that grow well together in each zone. Some plants are suggested in large masses that cover the ground, others as solitary or periodic accents to replicate a natural community. Others are plants that can provide shade to suppress weeds, retain moisture, or provide numerous other benefits for your garden. You will need to do some trimming to prevent, for example, your pōhinahina from overtaking and crowding out your ʻukiʻuki, but the intention is that over time, you may be able to be less and less involved.

As a user of this guide, it's not necessary that you completely dig up your yard and re-plant it with 100% natives. We recognize that many people may want to test the waters by initially planting just a few native Hawaiian plants or just a small section of their yard with natives. Perhaps you have a stately mango tree that provides delicious fruit like clockwork every year. Who would want to give that up? Rather than cutting down your mango tree, you could just plant a native Hawaiian ground cover and shrubs around and under it, leaving the mango tree where it is. That's perfectly acceptable and your choice. The point is to start wherever you are and evolve as you wish.

A Diamond Head residence. Design by Rick Quinn.

Native Hawaiian Plants are Underrated

In moving towards the use of more native Hawaiian plants in our landscaping it may be helpful to remember that native Hawaiian plants have many advantages over non-native plants. Many native Hawaiian plants require very little maintenance and little or no use of herbicides or fertilizer (some experts explicitly advise NOT to fertilize native Hawaiian plants), for example. Aside from saving you time and money, reducing or eliminating the use of herbicides, pesticides, and fertilizers can reduce your environmental footprint. Native Hawaiian plants are also potentially an excellent response to climate change and a world where water may become in increasingly short supply. The closure of the Hālawa well on Oʻahu and potential contamination of the aquifer add extra urgency (at least on Oʻahu) to using plants that require less water. According to Heidi Leianuenue Bornhorst, author of *Growing Native Hawaiian Plants: A How-To Guide for the Gardener*, "many natives, especially those native to

coastal and dry forest areas will help reach Hawaiʻi's goal of reducing wasteful watering practices [by using xeriphitic or drought-tolerant landscaping]."

Contrary to common perception, there are native Hawaiian plants that, when planted in the appropriate growing zone, are very hardy and can survive in harsh conditions—such as the kīpuka in a lava flow. This is logical: native Hawaiian plants have adapted over several millennia to life in these islands. As climate change impacts the state, they may have a role to play. While we can't predict the future, we have tried to factor in the potential impact of climate change when making plant recommendations.

Conservation and the Urban Forest

Creating this guide turned out to be far more complex than initially imagined. Apart from the work of compiling it, we encountered both practical and ethical questions. For example, should we only present plants that are readily available from local nurseries? We do not want people to get excited about a particular plant only to discover it's nearly impossible to find. On the other hand, we also do not want to present a narrow palette of the same plants that would be used over and over to the point where native Hawaiian gardens become boring monoculture landscapes. We've tried to find the right balance by presenting combinations of plants that are diverse and exciting, yet for the most part readily available from local sources. Partly, we're hoping that this guide and people's demand for new and exciting plants may stimulate nurseries to offer an even wider assortment of plants.

An ethical question we wrestled with was what to do about endemism? As a place blessed with numerous unique ecosystems, Hawaiʻi is home to many endemic plants that are only found on one island or even in an isolated valley or mountaintop on one island. Given their uniqueness, many of these plants risk extinction. Our dilemma was: should we promote the use of plants that are endemic to one place in other locations or on other islands? This could help to preserve genetic material from the plant but also risk it spreading to places where it doesn't naturally occur. The worst case could be a plant hybridizing and "muddling" the genes of other related plant varieties such that they lose their uniqueness. We do our best in this publication to encourage people to use plants that are endemic to their area, but have generally taken the view that plants, particularly those planted in urban settings, are less likely to spread to natural forests. The benefits of preserving genetic material may outweigh the risks.

The Larger Picture: Nature Restored from Mauka to Makai

There was a time in Hawaiʻi Nei when nature stretched uninterrupted from mauka to makai. We'll never return to those days of pristine natural beauty—certainly not in densely populated urban areas of the "concrete jungle". This is the harsh reality that has perhaps led some people to view urban areas as a "lost cause" and as separate from upland forests and other protected natural areas. That is no surprise: up to 95% of Hawaiʻi's dryland forests have been destroyed, and only 40% of our mesic forest remain. Despite the widespread destruction and the temptation to throw one's hands up in frustration, we have come to realize that nature in urban areas is important. As Hawaiʻi's official Forest Action Plan states: "Our islands' ecosystems are more dramatically and intricately connected than those on continents. Because of these tight connections, integrating urban forest issues into landscape and island-wide management efforts is necessary."[1]

While we cannot go back to the days of the past—and, indeed, some people may not want to—the Hawaiʻi Forest Institute and our community partners believe that there is another way forward. With help from the Kaulunani Urban and Community Forestry Program of the DLNR Division of Forestry and Wildlife, we launched the Go Native: Growing a Native Hawaiian Urban Forest project. The project aims to promote the growing of native Hawaiian and "canoe" (Polynesian-introduced) plants by creating a series of videos and this guide.

The long term goal of this effort is to create a series of kīpuka or micro-forests within the urban and suburban core. Once we convince enough homeowners, renters,

"There was a time in Hawaiʻi Nei when nature stretched uninterrupted from *mauka* to *makai*."

businesses, and landscape architects to use more native Hawaiian and canoe plants in their landscaping, these native gardens can collectively become a human-made surrogate for the natural forests that once existed in abundance, particularly in dryland and mesic areas. Within a generation, we can create a Native Hawaiian Urban Forest Network.

The Native Hawaiian Urban Forest Network would offer innumerable benefits to Hawaiʻi's people and to the ʻāina such as providing a refuge for native animals; wildlife corridors for native invertebrates, birds, and bats; preserving genetic variation within plant and animal species; and enhancing cultural and spiritual links with the past. Creating the Native Hawaiian Urban Forest Network could also help to increase the redundancy, representation, and resiliency of existing natural forests. If we build a Native Hawaiian Urban Forest Network of sufficient size and density, native birds and insects may even be able to extend their current ranges.

Imagine a Hawaiʻi in which no more native Hawaiian plants were to be found. So far, we've spoken of the practical aspects of growing native Hawaiian plants, but there is another reason why they are important. They connect us with the past, present, and future and are our roots in the ʻāina. By cultivating native Hawaiian plants, we also have an opportunity to cultivate a deeper connection with this place we call home.

---

[1] Hawaiʻi Forest Action Plan 2016, Department of Land and Natural Resources Division of Forestry and Wildlife Honolulu, Hawaiʻi December 31, 2016.

He keiki aloha nā mea kanu.

Beloved children are the plants.

ʻŌlelo Noʻeau no. 684, Mary Kawena Pukui.

Chapter Two

The maps that follow are based on the work of co-author Dr. Jonathan Price, along with Dr. Sam Gon (see his foreword) and others' research to map the natural geographic ranges of native Hawaiian plant species (Price et al. 2012). The zones are **arid** (having little to no rain), **dry, mesic** (a moderate amount of moisture) and **wet**. These terms are used rather than precipitation ranges, because the zones are based on a 'moisture availability index' that incorporates mean annual precipitation, potential evapotranspiration (factoring in temperature), and elevation. Additionally, many native Hawaiian plants only occur along coastal areas, so a coastal layer of ⅓ of a mile (500 meters) from the coastline was created. The above work resulted in 8 zones:

- Coastal Arid
- Coastal Dry
- Coastal Mesic
- Coastal Wet
- Inland Arid
- Inland Dry
- Inland Mesic
- Inland Wet

To learn more about the research that went into developing these zones (and their broader utility for plant conservation work) see *Mapping Plant Species Ranges in the Hawaiian Islands – Developing a Methodology and Associated GIS Layers* (Price et al. 2012).

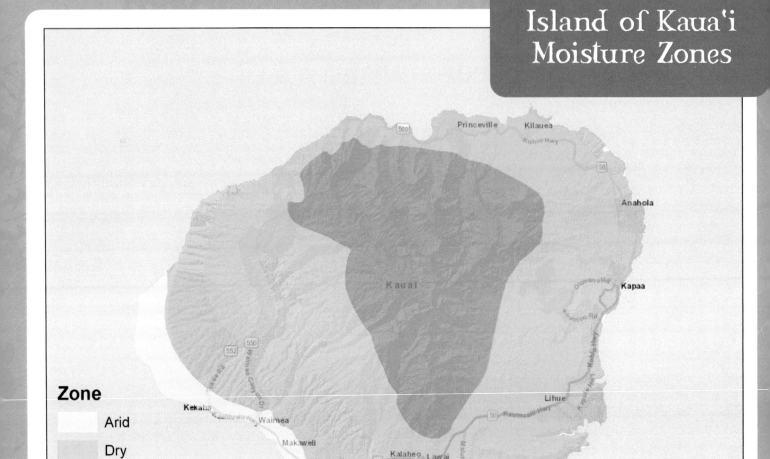

Island of Kaua'i Moisture Zones

Zone

Arid

Dry

Mesic

Wet

Princeville   Kilauea

Kuhio Hwy

Anahola

Kauai

Kapaa

Olomea Rd

Kamoo Rd

Lihue

Kekaha

Kaumualii Hwy   Waimea

Makaweli

Kaumakani

Kalaheo   Lawai

Koloa Rd

Hanapepe

Eleele   Kauai   Koloa

0   1.5   3   6   9   12   Miles

Sources: Esri, HERE, Garmin, USGS, Intermap, INCREMENT P, NRCan, Esri Japan, METI, Esri China (Hong Kong), Esri Korea, Esri (Thailand), NGCC. (c) OpenStreetMap contributors, and the GIS User Community

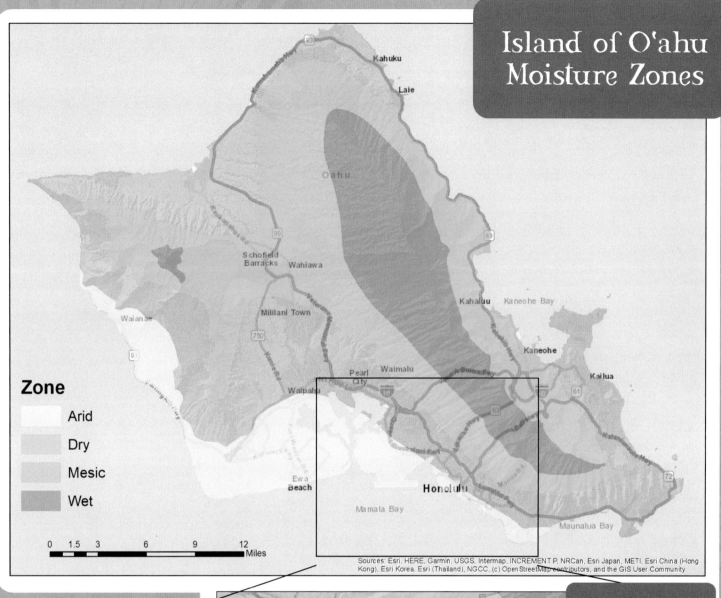

Island of O'ahu
Moisture Zones

Kahuku

Laie

Oahu

Schofield
Barracks   Wahiawa

Mililani Town

Waianae

Kahaluu   Kaneohe Bay

Kaneohe

Kailua

Pearl
City   Waimalu

Waipahu

Ewa
Beach   Honolulu

Mamala Bay

Maunalua Bay

Zone

Arid

Dry

Mesic

Wet

0   1.5   3   6   9   12
                                    Miles

Sources: Esri, HERE, Garmin, USGS, Intermap, INCREMENT P, NRCan, Esri Japan, METI, Esri China (Hong Kong), Esri Korea, Esri (Thailand), NGCC, (c) OpenStreetMap contributors, and the GIS User Community

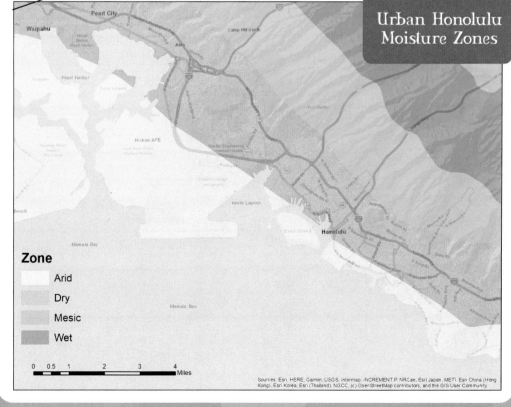

Urban Honolulu
Moisture Zones

Pearl City

Waipahu

Naval
Station
Pearl Harbor   Camp HM Smith

Aiea

Pearl Harbor

Ford Island

Hickam AFB

Keehi Lagoon

Beach

Mamala Bay

Honolulu

Mamala Bay

Zone

Arid

Dry

Mesic

Wet

0   0.5   1   2   3   4
                                    Miles

Sources: Esri, HERE, Garmin, USGS, Intermap, INCREMENT P, NRCan, Esri Japan, METI, Esri China (Hong Kong), Esri Korea, Esri (Thailand), NGCC, (c) OpenStreetMap contributors, and the GIS User Community

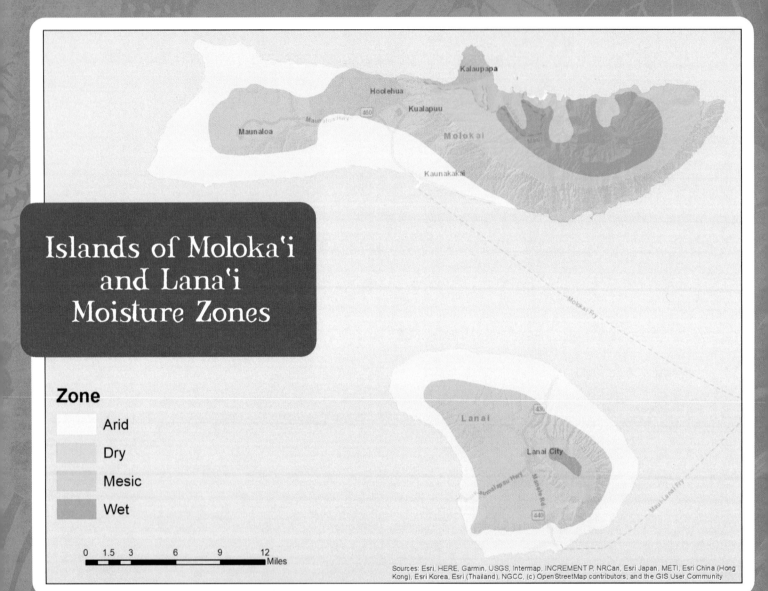

Islands of Moloka'i
and Lana'i
Moisture Zones

Zone

Arid
Dry
Mesic
Wet

0 1.5 3   6   9   12
                        Miles

Sources: Esri, HERE, Garmin, USGS, Intermap, INCREMENT P, NRCan, Esri Japan, METI, Esri China (Hong Kong), Esri Korea, Esri (Thailand), NGCC, (c) OpenStreetMap contributors, and the GIS User Community

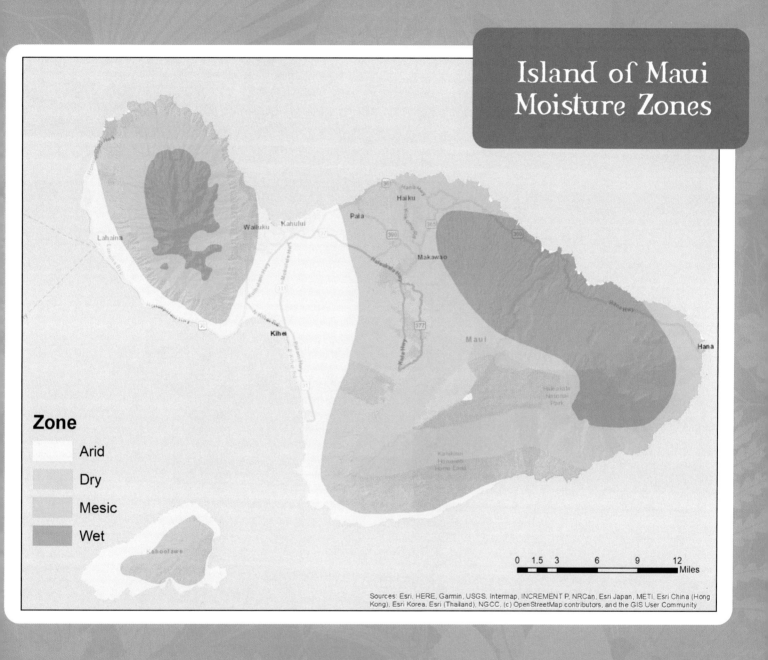

Island of Maui
Moisture Zones

Zone

- Arid
- Dry
- Mesic
- Wet

0 1.5 3   6   9   12
Miles

Sources: Esri, HERE, Garmin, USGS, Intermap, INCREMENT P, NRCan, Esri Japan, METI, Esri China (Hong Kong), Esri Korea, Esri (Thailand), NGCC, (c) OpenStreetMap contributors, and the GIS User Community

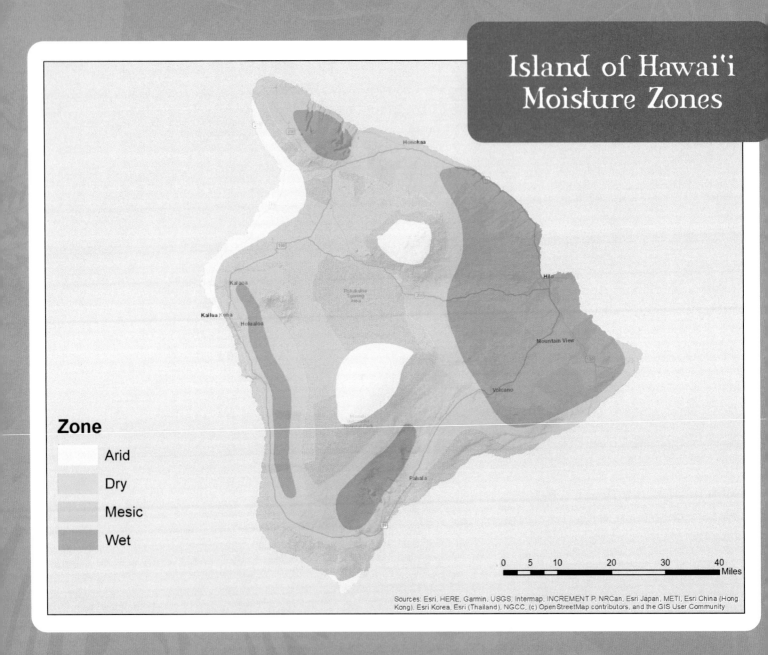

Island of Hawai'i
Moisture Zones

Honokaa

Hilo

Kalaoa

Kailua Kona

Holualoa

Pohakuloa
Training
Area

Mountain View

Volcano

Pahala

Zone

Arid

Dry

Mesic

Wet

0   5   10   20   30   40
                                    Miles

Sources: Esri, HERE, Garmin, USGS, Intermap, INCREMENT P, NRCan, Esri Japan, METI, Esri China (Hong Kong), Esri Korea, Esri (Thailand), NGCC, (c) OpenStreetMap contributors, and the GIS User Community

Chapter Three

The Quick Reference Table contains 216 plants and is designed to be self-explanatory, but the following information may help orient you and provide more details to aid interpretation.

Organization

The table contains 216 plants: 20 canoe plants and 196 native Hawaiian plants. Plant names are in green, black, or red.

Green: Canoe plants, or those brought by early Polynesian voyagers over 1,000 years ago.

Black: Native Hawaiian plants that came by wing (birds stomach or attached to feathers or muddy feet), wind (ferns and plants with small seeds), or water (seeds that can float, like naupaka kahakai).

Red: Native Hawaiian plants that have a special status (listed as federally endangered, threatened, or are categorized as vulnerable or on a watch list). Only plant these if available in the horticultural trade. Do not try to collect seeds from these on your own.

All plants (whether canoe plants or native Hawaiian plants) are sorted by form in the following order: Grasses (4), Sedges/rushes (15), Herbs (33), Ferns (12), Shrubs (78), Trees (60), and Vines (14).

Within the form, plants are sorted by common name. If you're wondering if a plant is in the table and you know its scientific name, but not its common name, go to the Index and it will indicate the form and the common name (as well as any designs it appears in).

Environmental Conditions: Right Plant, Right Place?

After names, the left side of the table (the columns on elevation through moisture level) includes factors to determine whether the environmental conditions of your site match what the plant is adapted to.

Arrows for elevation: Some plants naturally occur only at higher elevations, indicated with an arrow pointing up (the plants might struggle with higher temperature at lower elevations for example). Conversely, an arrow pointing down means these plants naturally occur only at lower elevation sites and they might struggle at elevations above 2,000 ft.

Salt tolerance: Y indicates the plant has some salt tolerance. However, there is variability in the level of tolerance. If your site is right up against the shore with regular and direct salt spray, a Y in this column does not necessarily mean the plant will be unharmed. Please refer to *Salt and wind tolerance of landscape plants for Hawaiʻi* (Bezona et al 2001) (https://www.ctahr.hawaii.edu/oc/freepubs/pdf/L-13.pdf) for more information.

Zones (Arid, Dry, Mesic and Wet in Coastal and Inland settings): As described in the introduction, plants are adapted to certain climates, particularly temperature and precipitation. Put a cactus in a rainforest, and it will be pretty unhappy. You may be wishing we just used precipitation ranges instead of terms like arid (having little to no rain), dry, mesic (a moderate amount

of moisture) and wet. The maps in the previous section are based on the "moisture availability index," which factors in both precipitation AND temperature. If you're working in the sun when it's 95 degrees out, you're going to need a lot more water to drink compared to when it's 70 degrees out. Plants are the same way and this zoning takes that into account.

Inland vs Coastal: Many native Hawaiian plants naturally occur only along the coast. The coastal layer is designated as land within ⅓ of a mile (500 meters) from the coastline. This doesn't mean all plants listed only in coastal zones like the shrub pōhinahina *(Vitex rotundifolia)* will do poorly inland, but that without human intervention, they are distributed coastally (and they should be used cautiously at notably high elevations as they wouldn't be adapted to colder temperatures). By contrast, we recommend being much more careful when considering plants listed only in inland zones for coastal sites as they will not be adapted to potential salinity there.

Zone flexibility? You'll note that some plants have a very wide range of adaptability like the tree milo *(Thespesia populnea)* which naturally occurs in all four coastal zones, compared to the tree hau hele ʻula *(Kokia drynarioides)* which naturally occurs only in the inland dry zone. Does this mean you can't plant hau hele ʻula in a mesic zone or an arid zone? We are encouraging you to choose plants that would naturally occur where you live. However, there is some room for flexibility. It depends on the plant and your property. If you're on the dry end of a mesic zone (situated closer to a dry zone than a wet zone), you'd probably be fine planting hau hele ʻula there.

Presence by Island: Some native plants are indigenous (are native to Hawaiʻi and elsewhere), endemic (native to Hawaiʻi and exist nowhere else), and some native plants naturally occur only on some islands! Choose species that naturally occur where you live whenever possible.

Sun: The symbols beneath full sun, partial sun and shade indicate what exposure levels each plant will tolerate. If a plant tolerates more than one exposure (e.g. full sun and partial sun), but has a preference for one (e.g. does best in full sun), both symbols would be shown, but full sun would be underlined.

Well-drained soil: Some plants don't like getting their "feet wet." They must have well-drained soil or they're prone to disease. If areas of your yard routinely form standing water after rain, that would not be a place for a plant indicated as needing well-drained soil.

Water: The moisture zones provide broad guidelines to help you select plants adapted to the moisture and humidity levels where you live. The table also includes water values on a scale of 1-5 to provide more specifics for each plant. However, an individual plant's needs depend on numerous factors including soils, seasonal weather, plant age, plant type (tree vs herb), and especially location (plants in hot urban settings with shallow soils and no surrounding vegetation to cool them will need more water than those in rural settings with established vegetation and deeper soils). These values are to provide rough guidelines, but you'll need to adapt your watering regime based on the specifics of your site.

> 1 = Extremely drought-tolerant (once established, would rarely need additional water)
>
> 2 = Accustomed to dry soils (in periods of drought, water 1-3x/month)
>
> 3 = Accustomed to moist but tolerates occasionally dry soil (in periods of drought, water 2-4x/month)
>
> 4 = Prefers continuously moist soils (plant where precipitation occurs regularly enough that soils are not dry)
>
> 5 = Needs very wet to moist soils and tolerates or thrives when submerged, like in a water feature

Notes: These values apply once the plant is established. No matter how drought-tolerant a plant might be, almost all plants need some additional watering initially to get established. This may be over 1-6 months depending on a number of factors such as the species, soil conditions, and seasonal climate at the time of planting. Start to reduce watering frequency and/or amount gradually, and monitor how the plant responds.

Plant Attributes: Right Plant for Your Landscaping Needs?

The right side of the table (columns on height, width and 10 columns on landscaping attributes) provides information to determine whether the plant is appropriate for your landscaping needs.

Height and Width: Height and width are provided to help plan for a given space. Please note some values are rough estimates as many native plants may vary considerably in size, often depending on where seeds were collected (check the comment section which may note this).

Landscape Attributes: Those that are not self explanatory are described below.

Accent: Plants which are ideal in periodic clusters to guide the eye and bring unity to the design.

Container plants: Plants that vary considerably in size are listed there with an X. A "C" after the X means the plant naturally occurs in cliff sites. This makes them especially well adapted to conditions in a shallow container. It also means they may be especially suited for windy conditions like those of a balcony in a high-rise building.

Ground cover: These are plants that are generally low growing (less than 3' tall) and often spread to help stop weeds from growing.

Specimen: In contrast to accent plants that are planted in numerous areas, specimens are typically planted as a single plant, and are "show stoppers," or have colorful flowers, unusual growth form, or some notable and attractive feature to draw attention to them.

Water feature: These are plants that tolerate high moisture levels and have attractive features making them suitable for the edge of a small pond or a constructed water feature.

Comments: Some plants have a (C) for challenging or an (S) for short lived. As noted, challenging plants are not recommended for novice gardeners, but people with more experience may be eager for this challenge (and willing to spend time learning about the plant's habitat and needs). Short-lived plants are equivalents to annuals. They are often great to fill in empty spaces while other plants develop, but shouldn't be used as core features of a design.

As noted in acknowledgements, we are deeply grateful for Native Plants Hawai'i (http://nativeplants.hawaii.edu/), and particularly the work of David Eickhoff for much of the information in this table.

Quick Reference Table

<table>
<tr>
<th rowspan="2">COMMON NAME</th>
<th rowspan="2">SCIENTIFIC NAME</th>
<th rowspan="2">prefers <2,000 ft</th>
<th rowspan="2">prefers >2,000 ft</th>
<th colspan="4">COASTAL</th>
<th colspan="4">INLAND</th>
<th rowspan="2">KAU'I</th>
<th rowspan="2">O'AHU</th>
<th rowspan="2">MOLOKA'I</th>
<th rowspan="2">LĀNA'I</th>
<th rowspan="2">MAUI</th>
<th rowspan="2">HAWAI'I</th>
<th rowspan="2">FULL SUN</th>
<th rowspan="2">PARTIAL SUN</th>
<th rowspan="2">SHADE</th>
<th rowspan="2">WELL DRAINED SOIL</th>
<th rowspan="2">IDEAL WATER (1-5*)</th>
<th rowspan="2">SALT TOLERANT</th>
</tr>
<tr>
<th>Arid (A)</th><th>Dry (D)</th><th>Mesic (M)</th><th>Wet (W)</th>
<th>Arid (A)</th><th>Dry (D)</th><th>Mesic (M)</th><th>Wet (W)</th>
</tr>

<tr><td>'Ama'u</td><td>*Sadleria cyatheoides*</td><td></td><td></td><td></td><td></td><td>M</td><td>W</td><td></td><td></td><td>M</td><td>W</td><td>X</td><td>X</td><td>X</td><td>X</td><td>X</td><td>X</td><td>○</td><td>◐</td><td></td><td>X</td><td>2-4</td><td></td></tr>

<tr><td>'Ama'u</td><td>*Sadleria pallida*</td><td></td><td></td><td></td><td></td><td></td><td></td><td></td><td></td><td>M</td><td>W</td><td>X</td><td>X</td><td>X</td><td>X</td><td>X</td><td>X</td><td></td><td>◐</td><td>●</td><td>X</td><td>3-4</td><td></td></tr>

<tr><td>'Ēkaha</td><td>*Asplenium nidus*</td><td></td><td></td><td></td><td></td><td></td><td></td><td></td><td></td><td>M</td><td>W</td><td>X</td><td>X</td><td>X</td><td>X</td><td>X</td><td>X</td><td></td><td>◐</td><td>●</td><td>X</td><td>3</td><td></td></tr>

<tr><td>Hāpu'u</td><td>*Cibotium chamissoi*</td><td></td><td></td><td></td><td></td><td></td><td></td><td></td><td></td><td>M</td><td>W</td><td></td><td>X</td><td>X</td><td>X</td><td>X</td><td>X</td><td></td><td>◐</td><td>●</td><td>X</td><td>4</td><td></td></tr>

<tr><td>Hāpu'u 'i'i</td><td>*Cibotium menziesii*</td><td></td><td></td><td></td><td></td><td></td><td></td><td></td><td></td><td>M</td><td>W</td><td>X</td><td>X</td><td>X</td><td>X</td><td>X</td><td>X</td><td></td><td>◐</td><td>●</td><td>X</td><td>4</td><td></td></tr>

<tr><td>Hāpu'u pulu</td><td>*Cibotium glaucum*</td><td></td><td></td><td></td><td></td><td></td><td></td><td></td><td></td><td>M</td><td>W</td><td>X</td><td>X</td><td>X</td><td>X</td><td>X</td><td>X</td><td>○</td><td>◐</td><td>●</td><td>X</td><td>4</td><td></td></tr>

<tr><td>'Ihi'ihi</td><td>*Marsilea villosa*</td><td>↓</td><td></td><td>A</td><td>D</td><td></td><td></td><td>A</td><td>D</td><td></td><td></td><td></td><td>X</td><td>X</td><td></td><td></td><td></td><td>○</td><td>◐</td><td></td><td></td><td>3-4</td><td></td></tr>

<tr><td>Kupukupu</td><td>*Nephrolepis cordifolia*</td><td></td><td></td><td></td><td></td><td></td><td></td><td></td><td></td><td>M</td><td>W</td><td>X</td><td>X</td><td>X</td><td>X</td><td>X</td><td>X</td><td>○</td><td>◐</td><td>●</td><td>X</td><td>3</td><td></td></tr>

<tr><td>Laukahi</td><td>*Cyclosorus hudsonianus*</td><td></td><td></td><td></td><td></td><td></td><td></td><td></td><td></td><td>M</td><td>W</td><td>X</td><td>X</td><td>X</td><td>X</td><td>X</td><td>X</td><td></td><td>◐</td><td>●</td><td></td><td>4</td><td></td></tr>

<tr><td>Moa</td><td>*Psilotum nudum*</td><td></td><td></td><td></td><td>D</td><td>M</td><td>W</td><td></td><td>D</td><td>M</td><td>W</td><td>X</td><td>X</td><td>X</td><td>X</td><td>X</td><td>X</td><td>○</td><td>◐</td><td>●</td><td>X</td><td>2-3</td><td></td></tr>

<tr><td>Neke</td><td>*Cyclosorus interruptus*</td><td></td><td></td><td></td><td>D</td><td>M</td><td>W</td><td></td><td>D</td><td>M</td><td>W</td><td>X</td><td>X</td><td>X</td><td>X</td><td>X</td><td>X</td><td>○</td><td>◐</td><td></td><td></td><td>4-5</td><td></td></tr>

<tr><td>Palapalai</td><td>*Microlepia strigosa* var. *strigosa*</td><td></td><td></td><td></td><td></td><td></td><td></td><td></td><td>D</td><td>M</td><td>W</td><td>X</td><td>X</td><td>X</td><td>X</td><td>X</td><td>X</td><td>○</td><td>◐</td><td>●</td><td>X</td><td>3-4</td><td></td></tr>

<tr><td>'Aki'aki</td><td>*Sporobolus virginicus*</td><td>↓</td><td></td><td>A</td><td>D</td><td>M</td><td>W</td><td></td><td></td><td></td><td></td><td>X</td><td>X</td><td>X</td><td>X</td><td>X</td><td>X</td><td>○</td><td></td><td></td><td>X</td><td>1-2</td><td>Y</td></tr>

<tr><td>Kāmano-mano</td><td>*Cenchrus agrimoniodes* var. *agrimoniodes*</td><td></td><td></td><td></td><td>D</td><td>M</td><td></td><td></td><td>D</td><td>M</td><td></td><td></td><td>X</td><td></td><td>X</td><td>X</td><td></td><td>○</td><td>◐</td><td></td><td>X</td><td>2-3</td><td></td></tr>

<tr><td>Kāwelu</td><td>*Eragrostis variabilis*</td><td></td><td></td><td>A</td><td>D</td><td>M</td><td>W</td><td></td><td>D</td><td>M</td><td>W</td><td>X</td><td>X</td><td>X</td><td>X</td><td>X</td><td>X</td><td>○</td><td></td><td></td><td>X</td><td>2</td><td>Y</td></tr>

<tr><td>Pili</td><td>*Heteropogon contortus*</td><td></td><td></td><td>A</td><td>D</td><td>M</td><td></td><td>A</td><td>D</td><td>M</td><td></td><td>X</td><td>X</td><td>X</td><td>X</td><td>X</td><td>X</td><td>○</td><td></td><td></td><td>X</td><td>1-3</td><td>Y</td></tr>
</table>

Section labels (vertical): FERN (rows 'Ama'u through Palapalai); GRASS (rows 'Aki'aki through Pili)

* 1. extremely drought tolerant (once established, would rarely need additional water); 2. accustomed to dry soils (in periods of drought, water 1-2/month once established); 3. accustomed to moist but tolerates occasionally dry; 4. prefers continuously moist soils; 5. wet to submerged (water feature)

Special status in red   Canoe in green

HEIGHT / WIDTH (feet)	ACCENT	CONTAINER: X CLIFF PLANT: C	GROUND COVER	HEDGE <5'	SCREEN >5'	SPECIMEN	TRELLIS/CLIMBER	SHADE COOLING	WATER FEATURE	FRAGRANT	COMMENTS (C)=challenging and for more experienced gardeners; (S)=short lived
1-5 / 4-6	X	X C									New leaves bright red, magenta, rust, and/or orange when fiddleheads (croziers) emerge to green upon maturity. At high altitudes it does fine in full sun, but needs more protection in urban areas. ʻAmaʻu tends to tolerate drier, sunnier places than hāpuʻu.
3-6 / 6-12	X	X									
2-4 / 1.5-3	X	X									Beautiful vase-shaped fern with large simple fronds that resemble banana leaves. Leaves are light green and wavy. Nice as an accent. Ok in dry zones with a bit more moisture.
2-10 / 8-10	X	X			X						Majestic ferns, great under trees to reduce erosion. Need slightly acidic, well-drained soil and plenty of moisture. *C. glaucum* is generally most common in the nursery trade and it does well in full sun only at higher elevations. Hawaiian honeycreepers use the pulu (wool) to line their nests. Feral pigs are an ongoing threat.
2-10 / 8-12	X	X			X						
2-8 / 8-10	X	X			X						
0.3-1 / 1+	X	X	X						X		(S) Unique fern with 4-leaf clover leaves. Easy to grow, spreads rapidly with periodic moisture. Rewatering may restore growth if it dries out.
1-3 / 1-4+	X	X	X								Excellent groundcover in sun and shade. Suitable in dry zones with a bit more moisture. Plants produce tubers (easy to propagate). Dense fronds control weeds. It will spread so be prepared to thin if paired with less dominant plants.
3-4 / 4	X	X	X								Lovely fronds are 2' long (trim spent fronds for a cleaner landscape appearance).
0.75-2.5 / 1.5	X	X C	X								(S) While not a true fern, and not the most ideal ground cover as it tends to pop up where it wants, valuable for its unique growth form.
1-2 / 1.5	X	X	X						X		Beautiful fern; plant in an area with regular moisture (like a downspout); fronds used to produce lei.
2-3 / 3-5	X	X	X							X	Stunning fern, easy to grow in partly sunny locations with sufficient moisture; great under trees as a high groundcover. Full sun ok with ample moisture and where not low elevation. Smells faintly of hay.
0.3-1.6 / 1-10+	X		X								Spreads if given room (not suitable as turf grass but considered for golf course roughs). Use as groundcover or for erosion control. Drought-tolerant, but needs regular water until established.
1-2.3 / 1-3		X	X								Easy to grow grass with unusual seed that makes a nice groundcover in full to partial sun.
1.3-2.6 / 1-3	X	X C	X								Great plant to fill in gaps or plant en masse to reduce erosion in sand or soil. Clumping (not rhizomatous) so shouldn't need edging to keep from spreading.
1.3-5 / 1.5-3	X		X	X						X	Adaptable bunchgrass makes a nice accent plant in dry sunny areas. Drought-tolerant, but will green up nicely with regular water. Tall and shorter forms available.

	COMMON NAME	SCIENTIFIC NAME	prefers <2,000 ft ↓	prefers >2,000 ft ↑	COASTAL Arid (A)	Dry (D)	Mesic (M)	Wet (W)	INLAND Arid (A)	Dry (D)	Mesic (M)	Wet (W)	KAU'I	O'AHU	MOLOKA'I	LĀNA'I	MAUI	HAWAI'I	FULL SUN	PARTIAL SUN	SHADE	WELL DRAINED SOIL	IDEAL WATER (1-5*)	SALT TOLERANT
SEDGE/RUSH	'Ahu'awa	*Cyperus javanicus*			A	D	M	W		D	M		X	X	X	X	X	X	○	◐			2-4	Y
	'Aka'akai	*Schoenoplectus tabernaemontani*			A	D	M	W				W	X	X	X			X	○	◐			5	Y
	Forked fimbry	*Fimbristylis dichotoma*	↓			D	M	W			M	W	X	X	X	X	X	X	○	◐			2-4	
	Hawai'i sedge	*Carex alligata*									M	W	X	X	X		X	X	○	◐			4-5	
	Kaluhā	*Schoenoplectiella juncoides*									M	W	X				X		○				4-5	
	Kaluhā	*Bolboschoenus maritimus*	↓		A	D							X	X	X		X	X	○	◐			4-5	Y
	Kohekohe	*Eleocharis erythropoda*	↓		A	D								X					○				4-5	Y
	Kohekohe	*Eleocharis obtusa*					M	W			M	W	X	X	X		X	X	○	◐			4-5	
	Makaloa	*Cyperus laevigatus*			A	D								X	X		X		○	◐			4-5	Y
	Mau'u 'aki'aki	*Fimbristylis cymosa*	↓		A	D	M	W	A	D	M		X	X	X	X	X	X	○	◐		X	1-3	Y
	Meyen's sedge	*Carex meyenii*									M	W	X	X	X	X	X	X	○	◐		X	2-3	
	O'ahu sedge	*Carex wahuensis* subsp. *wahuensis*				D	M	W		D	M	W	X	X	X	X	X	X	○	◐	●	X	2-3	
	Pu'uka'a	*Cyperus trachysanthos*			A	D			A	D			X	X	X				○	◐			4-5	Y
	'Uki	*Cladium jamaicense*			A	D	M	W			M	W	X	X	X		X	X	○	◐			4-5	Y
	'Uki	*Machaerina angustifolia*									M	W	X	X	X	X	X	X	○	◐			3-4	
HERB	Ae'ae	*Bacopa monnieri*	↓		A	D	M	W					X	X	X	X	X	X	○	◐			3-5	Y
	'Ākulikuli	*Sesuvium portulacastrum*	↓		A	D	M	W					X	X	X	X	X	X	○				2-5	Y
	'Ala'ala wai nui	*Peperomia blanda* var. *floribunda*				D	M			D	M	W	X	X	X	X	X	X		◐	●	X	2-3	
	'Ala'ala wai nui	*Peperomia mauiensis*									M	W			X	X	X			◐			3	
	'Ala'ala wai nui	*Peperomia sandwicensis*									M	W	X	X	X					◐		X	3	
	'Ala'ala wai nui	*Peperomia tetraphylla*								D	M	W	X	X	X	X	X	X		◐		X	2-3	

* 1. extremely drought tolerant (once established, would rarely need additional water); 2. accustomed to dry soils (in periods of drought, water 1-2/month once established); 3. accustomed to moist but tolerates occasionally dry; 4. prefers continuously moist soils; 5. wet to submerged (water feature)

Special status in red Canoe in green

HEIGHT — WIDTH (feet)	ACCENT	CONTAINER: X CLIFF PLANT: C	GROUND COVER	HEDGE <5'	SCREEN >5'	SPECIMEN	TRELLIS/CLIMBER	SHADE COOLING	WATER FEATURE	FRAGRANT	COMMENTS (C)=challenging and for more experienced gardeners; (S)=short lived
1.3-3.6 / 2	X	X	X						X		Attractive seed heads and bluish green foliage. Flood tolerant, good for erosion control and restoration. Native waterfowl use for food and nesting. Note: blades are sharp.
2.3-10 / 4-8+		X		X	X				X		Great screen or hedge for water features. Grow directly in water or in very moist conditions. Forms critical habitat for native and migratory waterfowl.
0.3-2.3 / 1	X	X	X								Nice accent or ground cover. Tolerates dry to moist conditions.
2-5 / 2	X	X	X								LIke Oʻahu sedge, but better for moister conditions and blades less sharp.
0.5-2.5 / 1	X	X	X						X		Attractive rush for water features or in pots with good moisture and sunlight. Use in routinely wet areas.
1-5 / 2	X	X	X						X		Great for reconstructing wetlands, provides food and shelter for native waterfowl. Spreads 1-2' to form a dense mass.
0.3-2 / +1	X	X	X						X		Great for water features or wet areas. Spreads >1' and considered aggressive so plant where it's desirable to spread.
0.2-1.3 / +1	X	X	X						X		Attractive, water-loving rush for small water features and in pots. Useful to reduce erosion, but may be overwhelmed by larger species like makaloa (*Cyperus laevigatus*) and kohekohe (*Eleocharis erythropoda*).
0.3- 1.5 / 8	X	X	X						X		Nice for small water features and to control erosion along stream banks. Provides food and shelter for native water birds.
0.2-2 / 0.5	X	X	X								Excellent drought-tolerant alternative to mondo grass in sunny areas. Use between paving stones in lightly used pathways. Don't overwater; soak and allow it to dry between watering.
1-2.3 / 2	X	X	X								Nice accent under tall shrubs or trees and in full sun, and attractive as a groundcover when planted en masse. Blades are a bit less sharp than Oʻahu sedge (*C. wahuensis*).
0.5-3.3 / 2	X	X	X								Attractive and tough. Nice accent or used en masse. Great alternative to non-native Umbrella sedge (*Cyperus alternifolius*). Leaf blades are sharp.
0.7-1.5 / 1	X	X	X						X		Handsome as specimen or planted en masse; lovely addition to Japanese-style gardens; leaves not as sharp as some other sedges.
3-6 / 4	X	X			X				X		Excellent sedge for natural settings. Needs wet soils or root mass submerged in water. Leaves have sharp edges.
1-4 / 3	X										Tall bullrush makes a nice accent plant; culturally used to make quick temporary mats or as bedding. Challenging to establish if not provided enough sun and moisture, but otherwise easy.
0.2-0.3 / 2+	X	X	X						X		Grow in wet soils or directly in water, but can also grow between stepping stones in moist soils.
0.3-0.8 / 3+	X	X	X						X		Extremely salt tolerant, excellent ground cover for beaches, saline soils and dry sites. Tolerates light foot traffic.
0.5-1 / 1-2	X	X C	X								
0.5-0.75 / 1	X	X	X								Peperomia are generally too slow growing to fill in as reliable ground covers but they do great as accents or in pots in partially shady locations. *P. blanda* and *P. tetraphylla* are more drought-tolerant and resistant to thrips. *P. sandwicensis* has lovely foliage (but very slow growing). All are generally pretty pest resistant, but watch for slugs.
0.5-0.8 / 1	X	X	X								
0.5-0.8 / 1-2	X	X	X								

COMMON NAME	SCIENTIFIC NAME	Elev. (↓<2,000ft / ↑>2,000ft)	Coastal Arid (A)	Coastal Dry (D)	Coastal Mesic (M)	Coastal Wet (W)	Inland Arid (A)	Inland Dry (D)	Inland Mesic (M)	Inland Wet (W)	KAU'I	O'AHU	MOLOKA'I	LĀNA'I	MAUI	HAWAI'I	FULL SUN	PARTIAL SUN	SHADE	WELL DRAINED SOIL	IDEAL WATER (1-5*)	SALT TOLERANT
'Ala'ala wai nui wahine	*Plectranthus parviflorus*		A	D			A	D			X	X	X	X	X	X	○	◐	●	X	2-3	Y
Alena, nena	*Boerhavia repens*	↓	A	D			A	D			X	X	X	X	X	X	○			X	1-2	Y
'Ānaunau	*Lepidium bidentatum var. o-waihiense*			D	M			D	M		X	X	X	X	X	X	○	◐		X	2-3	Y
'Awapuhi	*Zingiber zerumbet*				M	W			M	W	X	X	X	X	X	X		◐	●	X	3-5	
'Ihi	*Portulaca lutea*		A	D	M						X	X	X	X	X	X	○			X	1-2	Y
'Ihi	*Portulaca molokiniensis*	↓	A				A								X		○			X	1-2	Y
'Ihi	*Portulaca villosa*		A				A	D				X	X	X	X	X	○			X	1-2	Y
'Ilie'e	*Plumbago zeylanica*	↓	A	D			A	D	M		X	X	X	X	X	X	○	◐		X	1-2	
Kalo	*Colocasia esculenta*				M	W			M	W	X	X	X	X	X	X	○	◐	●		3-5	
Kolokolo kahakai	*Lysimachia mauritania*	↓		D	M	W					X		X		X	X	○	◐		X	2-3	Y
Kō'oko'olau	*Bidens amplectans*	↓						D				X					○	◐		X	2-3	
Kō'oko'olau	*Bidens hawaiensis*								M						X		○	◐		X	2-3	
Kō'oko'olau	*Bidens hillebrandiana*	↓			M	W								X	X	X	○	◐		X	2-3	Y
Kō'oko'olau	*Bidens micrantha* subsp. *micrantha*							D	M	W				X	X	X	○	◐		X	2-3	
Kō'oko'olau	*Bidens torta*							D	M	W		X					○			X	2-3	
Manono	*Kadua littoralis*	↓		D	M	W					X	X	X		X	X	○	◐		X	2-3	Y
Mau'u lā'ili	*Sisyrinchium acre*	↑							M	W					X	X	○	◐		X	2-4	
Nehe	*Lipochaeta integrifolia*	↓	A	D				D			X	X	X	X	X	X	○	◐		X	1-2	Y
Nohu	*Tribulus cistoides*	↓	A	D							X	X	X	X	X	X	○			X	1-2	Y

HERB

* 1. extremely drought tolerant (once established, would rarely need additional water); 2. accustomed to dry soils (in periods of drought, water 1-2/month once established); 3. accustomed to moist but tolerates occasionally dry; 4. prefers continuously moist soils; 5. wet to submerged (water feature)

Special status in red   Canoe in green

HEIGHT / WIDTH (feet)	ACCENT	CONTAINER: X CLIFF PLANT: C	GROUND COVER	HEDGE <5'	SCREEN >5'	SPECIMEN	TRELLIS/CLIMBER	SHADE COOLING	WATER FEATURE	FRAGRANT	COMMENTS (C)=challenging and for more experienced gardeners; (S)=short lived
0.3-2.5 / 1-2	X	X	X								(S) Looks best with some shade and adequate moisture; trim new growth, avoid cutting hard wood. Short-lived, but will reseed.
0.1-0.2 / 0.5			X								Pink flowers are lovely. Can form a fairly dense ground cover even in the light shade of trees.
0.5-2 / 1.5		X C	X							X	Early Hawaiians ate leaves raw or cooked, and it's used medicinally in other parts of Polynesia.
2-5 / 3->5	X	X		X						X	Stunning flowers. Dies back for ~3 months/year so avoid featuring as a specimen. Spreads (slowly) and can take over an area. Traditionally and currently used as a shampoo (directly or processed).
0.25-1 / 1	X	X C	X								Lovely succulent. Space 8-10" apart as ground cover; adequate drainage critical to prevent root rot.
0.5-1.5 / 0.8-1.6	X	X C	X								Great in pots, but full sun and excellent drainage essential (terracotta better than plastic). Has succulent, imbricate (stacked) leaves and stocky, upright growth.
0.25-0.75 / 2	X	X C	X								Full sun and excellent drainage are essential or will become leggy and prone to fungus. More prostrate than *Portulaca molokiniensis*.
1.5-6 / 2.5-5+	X	X	X	X							Great groundcover and soil stabilizer. Use in place of wedelia or non-native plumbago. Full sun is ideal, but tolerates shade better than many other drought-tolerant plants.
3->6 / 2-4+	X	X									A staple and staff of life in Hawaiian culture, providing nutritious food (both corms and leaves). Numerous varieties, some more tolerant of drier conditions and some tolerant of full shade: pick a variety based on your location.
0.3-3 / 1-2	X	X C	X								(S) Plant 6-10" apart for a nice groundcover in moist areas. Short-lived, but will reseed.
1.5-4 / 1.5-5	X	X C									Flowers larger than other *Bidens*. Trim for tidier appearance. Space 4-6' apart.
2-6 / 2-8	X	X C									Colorful yellow flowers. Naturally has a nice shape, but can be trimmed if it gets unruly.
0.6-1 / 0.6-1	X	c	X								Colorful yellow flowers. The latin name Bidens is appropriate given the two (bi) teeth (dens) that form on the seed structure.
1.5-5 / 2	X	X	X								Blooms continually in summer and sporadically year round; space 2' apart.
3.3-6 / 2.5-6	X	X									Colorful yellow flowers, highly variable in form. This and other *Bidens* used to make tea.
0.8-1.3 / 0.5-1		X C	X								(S) Bright white flowers make a showy display in pots or as a groundcover.
0.5-1 / 1.5	X										(S) Accustomed to higher elevations, but can grow as low as 300' in partial to full sun. Short-lived, but will re-seed.
0.3-1 / 3-6+	X	X	X								Succulent leaves and yellow daisy-like flowers. Great groundcover in low traffic areas, in rock gardens or spilling over walls.
0.2-0.7 / 1.6			X								(S) Sharp spiny seeds make it inappropriate where pets or anyone barefoot travels. Still a lovely native groundcover with yellow flowers for some shoreline sites. Short-lived but reseeds and spreads.

	COMMON NAME	SCIENTIFIC NAME	prefers <2,000 ft (↓) / prefers >2,000 ft (↑)	COASTAL				INLAND				KAU'I	O'AHU	MOLOKA'I	LĀNA'I	MAUI	HAWAI'I	FULL SUN	PARTIAL SUN	SHADE	WELL DRAINED SOIL	IDEAL WATER (1-5*)	SALT TOLERANT
				Arid (A)	Dry (D)	Mesic (M)	Wet (W)	Arid (A)	Dry (D)	Mesic (M)	Wet (W)												
HERB	'Olena	*Curcuma longa*			D	M	W			M	W	X	X	X	X	X	X	○	◐		X	2-4	
	Pa'iniu	*Astelia menziesiana*	↑							M	W	X	X	X	X	X	X		◐	●	X	3-4	
	Pia	*Tacca leontopetaloides*	↓		D	M	W		D	M	W	X	X	X	X	X	X	○	◐	●	X	2-3	Y
	Po'olā nui	*Bidens cosmoides*				M						X						○	◐		X	2-3	
	Pōpolo	*Solanum americanum*			D	M				M		X	X	X	X	X	X	○	◐		X	2-3	
	Pua kala	*Argemone glauca*		A	D	M		A	D	M		X	X	X	X	X	X	○			X	1-2	Y
	Sprawling schiedea	*Schiedea hookeri*							D	M	W	X				X			◐		X	2-3	
	'Uki'uki	*Dianella sandwicensis*				M	W			M	W	X	X	X	X	X	X	○	◐		X	2-4	Y
	'A'ali'i	*Dodonaea viscosa*		A	D	M			D	M	W	X	X	X	X	X	X	<u>○</u>	◐		X	1-2	Y
SHRUB	'Ahinahina	*Achyranthes splendens var. rotundata*		A	D	M		A	D	M			X	X	X			○			X	1-2	Y
	'Ahinahina	*Achyranthes splendens var. splendens*		A	D	M		A	D	M					X	X		○			X	1-2	Y
	'Āhinahina	*Artemisia australis*		A	D	M	W		D	M		X	X	X	X	X	X	○			X	1-2	Y
	'Āhinahina	*Artemisia mauiensis*	↑							M						X		○			X	2	
	'Ākala	*Rubus hawaiensis*	↑						D	M	W	X		X			X	○	◐		X	3	
	'Ākia	*Wikstroemia monticola*							D	M						X		○			X	2	
	'Ākia	*Wikstroemia oahuensis*							D	M	W	X	X	X	X	X		<u>○</u>	◐		X	2-4	
	'Ākia	*Wikstroemia uva-ursi*	↓		D	M			D	M		X	X	X		X		○			X	2	Y
	'Akiohala	*Hibiscus furcellatus*	↓							M	W	X	X			X	X	<u>○</u>	◐			3-5	
	'Akoko	*Euphorbia celastroides var. celastroides*		A	D	M		A	D	M		X	X	X	X	X	X	○			X	1-3	Y

* 1. extremely drought tolerant (once established, would rarely need additional water); 2. accustomed to dry soils (in periods of drought, water 1-2/month once established); 3. accustomed to moist but tolerates occasionally dry; 4. prefers continuously moist soils; 5. wet to submerged (water feature)

Special status in red Canoe in green

HEIGHT / WIDTH (feet)	ACCENT	CONTAINER: X / CLIFF PLANT: C	GROUND COVER	HEDGE <5'	SCREEN >5'	SPECIMEN	TRELLIS/CLIMBER	SHADE COOLING	WATER FEATURE	FRAGRANT	COMMENTS (C)=challenging and for more experienced gardeners; (S)=short lived
1.5-5 / 3+	X	X	X							X	Gorgeous flowers and medicinal benefits (roots are the source of turmeric, prized as an anti-inflammatory). Plant rhizomes 4" deep. Plants will go dormant during the dry season.
1-3 / 1-3	X	X C									(C) Stunning plants can grow in pots, or directly on hāpu'u ferns. An easy container plant, but may be more challenging in the landscape.
2-3 / 3	X	X									Has very attractive foliage and flowers. Produces an edible starch, used to make haupia, coconut pudding.
3-6 / 2.5-6	X	X									Large flowers are great for leis and blooms almost year round. Prune to make it more compact.
1-4 / 4	X	X									Decorative blackish purple fruits follow the flowers; easily grown in pots; easy to start from seed; considered essential for the Hawaiian herb garden.
2-5 / 0.75-2	X	XC		X							(S) Gorgeous white and yellow flowers, and blue gray foliage (with spiny prickles).
1-1.6 / 1-3	X	XC	X								(S,C) Will tolerate full sun, but best in partial shade; most Schiedea species naturally grow in north-facing habitats. Space 1-2 feet apart for a nice groundcover.
1.6-4 / 1-3	X	XC	X								Decorative purple (occasionally white) berries follow beautifully delicate flowers. Excellent groundcover or accent and does well in pots.
6.5-26 / 5-15	X	X	X	X	X	X					Tough, reliable, and beautiful shrub with decorative seed capsules (cream to red). Requires little care. Use it to stabilize slopes. May also grow as a tree.
1.5-6.5 / 2-5	X			X	X						Striking silvery-colored shrub with a spiky ball shape. Once established, avoid overwatering. Flower spikes and new leaves used in wili and haku lei.
1.5-6.5 / 2-5	X				X						Small shrub with green to silvery leaves.
2-10 / 3-4	X	X C		X						X	Drought-tolerant small to medium aromatic shrub with small, yellow flowers; silvery foliage adds a great color contrast.
1.5-6 / 3-4	X	X C	X							X	A small sprawling aromatic shrub with gray to silver leaves. Does well as an accent plant or en masse.
6-13 / 4-8	X				X						'Ākala, Hawaiian for pink, refers to the pinkish juice of this raspberry used to make dye for kapa (tapa). Great for nectar feeding birds like 'i'iwi (which eat the fruit too). Needs cooler temperatures, best above 1,000'.
6-10 / 4	X				X						A tough 'ākia that's great for dry, windy mid or low elevation, but not coastal. Forms a decorative orange berry.
4-20 / 4-10	X	X		X	X	X				X	An attractive 'ākia, easy to grow in urban gardens. Highly variable depending on origin; may grow as a prostrate shrub to small tree.
2-6 / 2-6	X	X C	X	X							Incredibly dependable, easy to grow plant with waxy green leaves, small yellowish green flowers and orange berries. Plant 2' on center for dense cover, further for a more naturalized look. Flowers, fruit, twigs prized for haku leis.
3.3-8 / 6		X		X	X				X		Long-lived native hibiscus can grow next to water features or even with roots submerged. Note: akilohala has irritating hairs on the stems and leaves.
3-12 / 6	X	X C	X	X		X					Long-lived small to medium shrub that makes a stunning accent plant or hedge.

Left vertical label: **SHRUB**

COMMON NAME	SCIENTIFIC NAME	prefers <2,000 ft ↓ / prefers >2,000 ft ↑	COASTAL Arid (A)	Dry (D)	Mesic (M)	Wet (W)	INLAND Arid (A)	Dry (D)	Mesic (M)	Wet (W)	KAU'I	O'AHU	MOLOKA'I	LĀNA'I	MAUI	HAWAI'I	FULL SUN	PARTIAL SUN	SHADE	WELL DRAINED SOIL	IDEAL WATER (1-5*)	SALT TOLERANT
'Akoko	Euphorbia degeneri	↓	A	D	M							X	X	X	X	X	○	◐		X	1-2	Y
Ālula	Brighamia insignis	↓			M				M		X						○			X	2	Y
'Ānapanapa	Colubrina asiatica	↓		D							X	X	X				○	◐		X	2-3	Y
Auhuhu	Tephrosia purpurea	↓	A	D	M	W		D	M		X	X	X	X	X	X	○			X	1-3	Y
'Āweoweo	Chenopodium oahuense		A	D	M		A	D	M		X	X	X	X	X	X	○	◐		X	1-2	Y
Hāhā	Clermontia clermontioides	↑							M	W						X		◐		X	4	
Hao	Rauvolfia sandwicensis							D	M		X	X	X	X	X	X	○	◐		X	2-3	
Hinahina	Heliotropium anomalum var. argenteum	↓	A	D							X	X	X		X	X	○			X	1-2	Y
Hōlei	Ochrosia haleakalae								M	W					X	X	○			X	2-3	
'Iliahialo'e	Santalum ellipticum	↓	A	D			A	D	M		X	X	X	X	X	X	○	◐		X	1-3	Y
Iliau	Wilkesia gymnoxiphium							D	M		X						○			X	2	
'Ilima	Sida fallax			D	M	W		D	M	W	X	X	X	X	X	X	○			X	2-3	Y
Kanawao	Hydrangea arguta	↑							M	W	X	X	X	X	X	X		◐		X	3-4	
Ki	Cordyline fruticosa		A	D	M	W		D	M	W	X	X	X	X	X	X	○	◐	●	X	3-4	
Ko	Saccharum officinarum			D	M	W			M	W	X	X	X	X	X	X	○			X	2-3	
Kōke'e yellow loosestrife	Lysimachia glutinosa	↑							M		X						○	◐		X	2-3	

* 1. extremely drought tolerant (once established, would rarely need additional water); 2. accustomed to dry soils (in periods of drought, water 1-2/month once established); 3. accustomed to moist but tolerates occasionally dry; 4. prefers continuously moist soils; 5. wet to submerged (water feature)

Special status in red Canoe in green

HEIGHT / WIDTH (feet)	ACCENT	CONTAINER: X CLIFF PLANT: C	GROUND COVER	HEDGE <5'	SCREEN >5'	SPECIMEN	TRELLIS/CLIMBER	SHADE COOLING	WATER FEATURE	FRAGRANT	COMMENTS (C)=challenging and for more experienced gardeners; (S)=short lived
0.2-1.3 / 1.5	X	X C	X								This small shrub adds a unique texture to the garden and will not become invasive like other non-native spurges.
2-3 / 2.75	X	X C								X	Stunning plant with unusual growth form and showy flowers. Easy to grow given partial sun and excellent drainage, whether in pots or in the ground (protect from slugs).
10-30 / 8	X	X		X	X						Drought-tolerant sprawling plant that needs room. It can overwhelm other native plants, but is useful as a filler.
1.3-5 / 0.75-3.5	X	X	X								(S) Great for low water use areas, but can look weedy. Has small purple flowers. Traditionally used to poison fish.
1.5-6.5 / 4-8	X	X		X							This partially woody plant with grayish leaves usually grows as a shrub, but a low growing form from Molokai is sometimes available. Its flowers can be distinctly scented.
5-20 / 3-12						X					(C) Hard to find, but a unique and beautiful plant if available.
10-32 / 10-21	X				X	X		X		X	A showy shrub. The flowers' fragrance is similar to plumeria.
0.3-1.3 / 2-5	X	X	X								Silvery foliage, white flowers form a beautiful ground cover, especially when planted near black cinder or rocks. Thrives in dry coastal landscapes. Flowers and leafy rosettes prized for haku leis.
6.5-26 / 8						X				X	Small flowers smell of plumeria. Easy to grow, and does well in the low, dry suburban areas (but not coastal). Availability limited (ideally will change as demand increases).
3-16 / 8-12	X				X	X		X		X	This shrub needs a host plant and although not choosy about which one, its health depends on healthy host plants (avoid herbicides in its vicinity). Flowers have a pleasant sandalwood scent.
3-16 / 3-8	X					X				X	Striking plant, easy to grow, and has ginger-scented leaves. Adapted to high elevation, but can grow near sea level. Dies after flowering, but the attractive growth form prior to flowering makes it worth it. Water weekly until established, then deep waterings only during drought.
0.7-5 / 2-6	X	X C	X	X	X	X					'Ilima papa is a low-growing, more drought-tolerant plant adapted to the lowlands. 'Ilima (as opposed to 'ilima papa) is upland, more upright and requires more water. Avoid automatic watering, especially in the drought-tolerant lowland forms or plants prone to disease.
5-16 / 8.75-28	X	X				X					(C) Related to cultivated hydrangeas, it produces beautiful flowers in a wide range of colors. Naturally occurring above 980' in cooler, high elevation wet forests, and occasionally mesic. Challenging for typical lowland landscapes and best as a container plant if attempted.
4-12 / 2-4	X	X		X	X	X					A reliable garden plant that can be a nice vertical accent in the garden or as a screen if planted densely. Has many traditional uses including wrappings for food and offerings, roof thatching, and hula skirts.
6-20 / 6	X				X						Native Hawaiians grew nearly 40 varieties of this plant, and used it to sweeten medicine and food. Some varieties are vibrantly colored, some "banded" or striped. Large biomass producer- stalks must be harvested or clumps will spread.
2-7 / 3-5	X	XC	X			X				X	This sprawling shrub has attractive fragrant bell-shaped flowers that last for a week or more.

SHRUB

Common Name	Scientific Name	prefers <2,000 ft	prefers >2,000 ft	Coastal Arid (A)	Coastal Dry (D)	Coastal Mesic (M)	Coastal Wet (W)	Inland Arid (A)	Inland Dry (D)	Inland Mesic (M)	Inland Wet (W)	KAUʻI	OʻAHU	MOLOKAʻI	LĀNAʻI	MAUI	HAWAIʻI	FULL SUN	PARTIAL SUN	SHADE	WELL DRAINED SOIL	IDEAL WATER (1-5*)	SALT TOLERANT
Kokiʻo keʻokeʻo	*Hibiscus arnottianus* subsp. *arnottianus*									M	W	X						○	◐		X	2-3	
Kokiʻo keʻokeʻo	*Hibiscus arnottianus* subsp. *immaculatus*									M	W			X				○	◐		X	3	
Kokiʻo keʻokeʻo	*Hibiscus arnottianus* subsp. *punaluuensis*									M	W	X						○	◐		X	3	
Kokiʻo kea	*Hibiscus waimeae* subsp. *hannerae*									M	W	X						○	◐		X	3	
Kokiʻo kea	*Hibiscus waimeae* subsp. *waimeae*									M	W	X						○	◐		X	3	
Kokiʻo ʻula	*Hibiscus clayi*	↓								M		X						○			X	2-3	
Kokiʻo ʻula	*Hibiscus kokio* subsp. *kokio*								D	M	W	X	X	X		X	X	○			X	2-3	
Kokiʻo ʻula	*Hibiscus kokio* subsp. *saintjohnianus*								D	M	W	X						○			X	2-3	
Kōlea lau liʻi	*Myrsine sandwicensis*									M	W	X		X	X	X	X	○	◐		X	2-4	
Kolokolo kauhiwi	*Lysimachia hillebrandii*								D	M	W	X	X	X	X	X		○	◐	●	X	2-3	
Kolokolo mokihana	*Melicope clusiifolia (Pelea clusiifolia)*									M	W	X	X	X	X	X	X	○	◐		X	3-4	
Kōʻokoʻolau	*Bidens menziesii* subsp. *filiformis*								D	M							X	○	◐		X	2	
Kōʻokoʻolau	*Bidens menziesii* subsp. *menziesii*								D	M				X		X		○	◐		X	2	
Koʻoloa ʻula	*Abutilon menziesii*	↓						A	D				X		X	X	X	○			X	1-2	
Kūkaenēnē	*Coprosma ernodeoides*		↑							M	W					X	X	○	◐		X	2	
Kuluʻī	*Nototrichium humile*								D	M			X			X		○	◐		X	2	
Kuluʻī	*Nototrichium sandwicense*			A	D	M			D	M		X	X	X	X	X	X	○			X	2	Y
Maiapilo	*Capparis sandwichiana*	↓		A	D	M		A	D			X	X	X	X	X	X	○			X	1-2	Y
Mamaki	*Pipturus albidus*									M	W	X	X	X	X	X	X		◐		X	2-3	
Maʻo	*Gossypium tomentosum*	↓		A	D			A				X	X	X	X	X		○			X	1-2	Y

* 1. extremely drought tolerant (once established, would rarely need additional water); 2. accustomed to dry soils (in periods of drought, water 1-2/month once established); 3. accustomed to moist but tolerates occasionally dry; 4. prefers continuously moist soils; 5. wet to submerged (water feature)

Special status in red Canoe in green

HEIGHT WIDTH (feet)	ACCENT	CONTAINER: X CLIFF PLANT: C	GROUND COVER	HEDGE <5'	SCREEN >5'	SPECIMEN	TRELLIS/CLIMBER	SHADE COOLING	WATER FEATURE	FRAGRANT	COMMENTS (C)=challenging and for more experienced gardeners; (S)=short lived
10-30 / 10-20		X C			X	X				X	
10-30 / 10-20					X	X				X	Beautiful shrubs with white flowers. Subspecies arnottianus has a red staminal column, others with white staminal column.
10-30 / 10-20		X C			X	X				X	
6-15 / 6-10+		X C			X	X				X	Beautiful shrub with attractive, fragrant white flowers, does well as a hedge or an accent plant. More resistant to hibiscus erineum mites that plague hibiscus hybrids. Some are very fragrant.
15-33 / 6-12+	X	X C			X	X		X		X	Beautiful shrub with attractive, fragrant white flowers, does well as a hedge or an accent plant. More resistant to hibiscus erineum mites that plague hibiscus hybrids. Some are very fragrant.
13-26 / 5-10	X	X			X	X					Compact long-lived shrub with attractive red flowers. Does well as an accent plant or hedge.
3-23 / 4-12	X	X C		X	X						Long-lived shrub or small tree does well as a background plant or in a pot.
3-23 / 4-12	X	X C		X	X						Attractive shrub with spectacular yellow to orange flowers.
5-13 / 3-6	X			X	X	X					(C) An amazing plant, but hard to find and not for the novice gardener. Needs regular watering and rich well-drained soil.
1.3-8 / 2-6	X	X C									A sprawling shrub with trumpet-shaped flowers.
6.5-33 / 4-20	X					X				X	(C) A great plant, but hard to find and best for experienced gardeners.
2.5-8 / 2-6	X	X C									While variable in size, it can get quite tall and classified as a shrub. Has attractive yellow flowers and does well as an accent plant or as a hedge. Note subspecies filiformis is on the Big Island and menziesii is on Moloka'i and Maui.
2.5-8 / 2-6	X	X									
6-10 / 2-4	X	X		X	X	X					Attractive shrubs with silvery-green foliage and beautiful flowers; excellent heat and drought tolerance once established. Avoid overwatering for best flower production.
0.5-6 / 10			X	X							Typically high elevation, but has done well lower down (100' windward Oahu). This long-lived sprawling shrub produces black jelly bean-shaped fruits prized by the endangered nene goose (common name means nene droppings).
3-15 / 10	X			X	X						New leaves are tinged pink and shimmer in the sun. Does well as a hedge or accent plant.
3-13 / 3-6	X	X		X	X	X					Great as an accent or hedge with silvery foliage. Wood used to make gunwales; bark, leaves and flowers used medicinally.
3.3-5 / 4-6	X		X	X	X	X				X	Stunning white or yellow flowers. Does well as an accent plant, or a low hedge.
6.5-20 / 6-10	X	X		X	X						Plant to attract native butterflies! This valuable shrub or small tree does well as an understory and has medicinal uses, especially as a tea.
1.5-5 / 5	X	X		X		X					Often called "Hawaiian cotton," a small to medium shrub with yellow flowers. Does well as an accent plant, in a hedge or a pot. A green dye can be obtained from the yellow flowers.

COMMON NAME	SCIENTIFIC NAME	prefers <2,000 ft ↓ / prefers >2,000 ft ↑	COASTAL				INLAND				KAU'I	O'AHU	MOLOKA'I	LĀNA'I	MAUI	HAWAI'I	FULL SUN	PARTIAL SUN	SHADE	WELL DRAINED SOIL	IDEAL WATER (1-5*)	SALT TOLERANT
			Arid (A)	Dry (D)	Mesic (M)	Wet (W)	Arid (A)	Dry (D)	Mesic (M)	Wet (W)												
Ma'o hau hele	*Hibiscus brackenridgei* subsp. *brackenridgei*	↓					A	D					X	X	X	X	○			X	2-3	
Ma'o hau hele	*Hibiscus brackenridgei* subsp. *mokuleianus*	↓					A	D				X					○			X	2-3	
Ma'o hau hele	*Hibiscus brackenridgei* subsp. *molokaiana*	↓					A	D				X	X				○			X	2-3	
Ma'oli'oli	*Schiedea globosa*	↓	A	D	M							X	X		X	X	○	◑		X	2	Y
Naio	*Myoporum stellatum*	↓	A				A					X					○			X	1-2	Y
Nā'ū	*Gardenia brighamii*	↓						D				X	X	X	X	X	○			X	2-3	
Naupaka, Dwarf	*Scaevola coriacea*	↓	A	D							X	X	X	X	X	X	○			X	1-3	Y
Naupaka kahakai	*Scaevola taccada*	↓	A	D	M	W					X	X	X	X	X	X	○			X	2	Y
Naupaka kuahiwi	*Scaevola chamissoniana*								M	W		X	X	X	X	X	○	◑		X	3-4	
Naupaka kuahiwi	*Scaevola gaudichaudiana*	↑							M	W	X	X						◑	●	X	2-3	
Naupaka kuahiwi	*Scaevola gaudichaudii*	↓	A	D			A	D			X	X	X	X	X	X	○			X	2-3	
Nene leau	*Rhus sandwicensis*								M	W	X	X	X		X	X	○	◑		X	3	
'Ōhā wai	*Clermontia kakeana*								M	W		X			X			◑		X	4	
'Oha	*Delissea rhytidosperma*								M	W	X							◑		X	2-3	
'Ōhā wai nui	*Clermontia arborescens*	↑							M	W			X	X	X		○	◑		X	4	
'Ohai	*Sesbania tomentosa*		A	D			A	D			X	X	X	X	X	X	○			X	1-2	Y
'Ohe (bamboo)	*Schizostachyum glaucifolium*				M	W			M	W	X	X	X	X	X	X	○			X	3-4	

SHRUB

* 1. extremely drought tolerant (once established, would rarely need additional water); 2. accustomed to dry soils (in periods of drought, water 1-2/month once established); 3. accustomed to moist but tolerates occasionally dry; 4. prefers continuously moist soils; 5. wet to submerged (water feature)

Special status in red   Canoe in green

HEIGHT / WIDTH (feet)	ACCENT	CONTAINER: X CLIFF PLANT: C	GROUND COVER	HEDGE <5'	SCREEN >5'	SPECIMEN	TRELLIS/CLIMBER	SHADE COOLING	WATER FEATURE	FRAGRANT	COMMENTS (C)=challenging and for more experienced gardeners; (S)=short lived
3-12 / 8		X		X	X	X					
3-12 / 8		X			X	X					Beautiful hibiscus and the state flower of Hawaiʻi. Common name means "green traveling hau," referring to how this sprawling plant may topple over, root at the nodes, and form a new plant. Periodic pruning will prevent this.
3-10 / 8-10		X		X	X	X					
0.3-1.3 / 3	X	X C	X							X	While individual flowers are inconspicuous, they are showy *en masse* and look great in containers and hanging baskets.
2-12 / 3-6	X	X		X	X					X	Nice replacement for the poisonous and similar looking oleander. Does well with native grasses such as pili. At time of printing, it is not widely available to limit spread of an invasive thrip.
6-15 / 6-12	X	X		X	X	X				X	Easy to grow shrubs or small trees with fragrant flowers. Does well as an accent plant, hedge or in a large pot. Slow growing, but well worth it.
0.3-2 / 2-4	X	X	X							X	Great for full sun, windy, dry conditions with salt spray. Easy to grow and with small fragrant flowers. Attractive groundcover or accent plant over rocks. Slow growing, but worth it.
1.5-10 / 10+	X	X	X	X	X					X	Most widely used of all native plants, great for low maintenance, dry areas. Excellent as an informal hedge, a filler and a windbreak.
4.5-8 / 6	X			X		X				X	This mountain naupaka is well adapted to cooler temperatures with wetter conditions and requires well-drained loam soil.
5-10 / 8	X	X C		X	X					X	This beautiful mountain naupaka does best with some shade, especially in late afternoon, but will tolerate full sun in cloudier, rainier areas. Forms a nice dense shrub and does well under taller trees. Though rather easy to grow, it can be more challenging than other *Scaevola* spp. to maintain (particularly susceptible to insect pests).
1.5-5 / 3-8	X		X	X						X	One of the easiest, hardiest and most rewarding naupakas, but can be hard to find. Best in full sun, thrives in harsh, dry, and windy locations.
9-27 / 6+	X					X					New leaves (liko) of this plant are striking, but the plant produces numerous root suckers and spreads aggressively. Plant to screen an unsightly feature or where you need something to fill in, but be mindful it can be difficult to control.
3-12 / 10						X					(C) Stunning flowers. Not difficult to grow as long as pests are controlled, especially during establishment.
2-8 / 3	X	X C				X					Easy-to-grow small to large shrubs with yellow flowers. Grows well in pots or in the ground with good drainage.
5-26 / 6						X					This shrub or small tree can take a beautiful form. It has showy flowers and orange berries.
2-3.5 / 2-3	X	X C	X	X		X				X	Stunning plant with beautiful flowers. Most nursery plants are sourced from low-growing plants (3' tall), but 'ohai is highly variable depending on origin (can be >15' and spread 10'+). Ask about the origin of plant material.
10-50 / 20					X						Many traditional uses, including as water carriers, musical instruments, and sharp tools. Use a clumping variety or will spread and take over.

COMMON NAME	SCIENTIFIC NAME	prefers <2,000 ft ↓ / prefers >2,000 ft ↑	COASTAL Arid (A)	Dry (D)	Mesic (M)	Wet (W)	INLAND Arid (A)	Dry (D)	Mesic (M)	Wet (W)	KAU'I	O'AHU	MOLOKA'I	LĀNA'I	MAUI	HAWAI'I	FULL SUN	PARTIAL SUN	SHADE	WELL DRAINED SOIL	IDEAL WATER (1-5*)	SALT TOLERANT
'Ōhelo 'ai	Vaccinium reticulatum	↑						D	M	W	X	X	X		X	X	○	◐		X	2-4	
'Ōhelo kai	Lycium sandwicense	↓	A	D	M						X	X	X	X	X	X	○			X	1-2	Y
'Ōhelo kau lā'au	Vaccinium calycinum	↑							M	W	X	X	X	X	X	X	○	◐		X	2-3	
Olonā	Touchardia latifolia				M	W			M	W	X	X	X	X	X	X			●	X	3-5	
Pamakani	Tetramolopium lepidotum subsp. lepidotum							D	M			X		X			○	◐		X	1-2	
Pawale	Rumex skottsbergii							D	M	W						X	○			X	2	
Pōhinahina	Vitex rotundifolia	↓	A	D	M	W					X	X	X	X	X	X	○	◐		X	1-3	Y
Pōpolo	Solanum nelsonii	↓	A	D							X	X	X		X	X	○			X	1-2	Y
Pōpolo	Solanum sandwicense								M	W	X	X					○	◐		X	2-3	
Pōpolo kū mai	Phytolacca sandwicensis								M	W	X	X	X		X	X		◐		X	2-4	
Pūkiawe	Leptecophylla tameiameiae			D	M	W		D	M	W	X	X	X	X	X	X	○			X	1-3	Y
Ridgetop tetra-molopium	Tetramolopium filiforme							D	M			X					○	◐		X	1-2	
'Uhaloa	Waltheria indica		A	D	M	W	A	D	M	W	X	X	X	X	X	X	○	◐		X	1-2	Y
'Ūlei	Osteomeles anthyllidifolia			D	M	W		D	M		X	X	X	X	X	X	○	◐		X	2	Y

SHRUB

* 1. extremely drought tolerant (once established, would rarely need additional water); 2. accustomed to dry soils (in periods of drought, water 1-2/month once established); 3. accustomed to moist but tolerates occasionally dry; 4. prefers continuously moist soils; 5. wet to submerged (water feature)

Special status in red Canoe in green

HEIGHT / WIDTH (feet)	ACCENT	CONTAINER: X CLIFF PLANT: C	GROUND COVER	HEDGE <5'	SCREEN >5'	SPECIMEN	TRELLIS/CLIMBER	SHADE COOLING	WATER FEATURE	FRAGRANT	COMMENTS (C)=challenging and for more experienced gardeners; (S)=short lived
0.34.3 / 0.2-3	X										(C) Attractive red, yellow, or striped bell-shaped flowers are followed by red, purple, dull black, yellow orange or even pink fruit making a showy display. Pinch and trim to encourage dense branching. It will struggle at lower, warmer elevations.
2-3.3 / 3-5		X	X								Great groundcover for low elevation and coastal sites, but also fine at higher elevations with good drainage. Thrives in sandy, rocky soil. Will flower and fruit a year from planting and produce decorative red berries.
3.3-10 / 6	X										(C) Common in uplands, but generally not suitable for a typical lowland urban landscape.
3-10 / 2-6	X										(C) Attracts the native Kamehameha butterfly (Vanessa tameamea). Avoid spraying insecticides on the plants. The fiber was used traditionally to make excellent rope, twine and thread.
0.4-1.2 / 1	X	X C				X					A rare and attractive small shrub, this plant needs regular water only for the first month or two and then only when soil is very dry.
3-6 / 2-4	X	X	X								Can be used as an accent plant, ground cover or grown in a pot. Has several traditional medicinal uses.
2-4 / 2-4	X	X C	X	X	X						Remarkably dependable, easy to grow groundcover or sprawling shrub, spreading laterally once established. Responds well to pruning. Has lovely flowers and sage/lavender scented leaves.
1-3.3 / 5	X	X	X	X		X	X				Growth habit varies (prostrate ground cover to small shrub) depending on the origin of parent plants. Purple berries are decorative, but fruit is not edible. If in pots moisture rating 1-2; in the ground: 1. Susceptible to rot and nematodes from excessive water (a nematicide to prevent root-knot nematodes may be helpful).
2-13 / 1.3-8	X	X									Growing as a shrub or small tree, has an unusual appearance and is recommended for native plant enthusiasts. Sadly, it's extremely rare, but will do well in full sun to partial shade with little water once established.
2.5-6 / 6-10	X	X	X								Infrequently used shrub but has potential for low to mid elevation gardens.
2-16 / 4-8	X	X C		X	X						(C) Common in undeveloped areas, but uncommon in urban landscapes as slow to germinate and grow. Leaves traditionally used for colds and headaches. Salt tolerance depends on origin of seeds.
0.2-0.5 / 1	X	X C				X					Beautiful flowers grace this small, rare shrub. Water weekly for 1st 1-2 months and then only when soil is very dry. Does well in pots, but well drained soil is critical.
1-3 / 1.5-4.5		X C								X	(S) While not prized ornamentally, this plant is common in undeveloped areas, and used in herb gardens where it's valued medicinally.
1.5-9 / 4-8	X	X C	X	X	X	X	X			X	Easy, drought-tolerant plant requires little maintenance. Forms white fragrant flowers. Overwatering will reduce flowering. Prostrate and upright forms available.

COMMON NAME	SCIENTIFIC NAME	prefers <2,000 ft (↓) / prefers >2,000 ft (↑)	COASTAL Arid (A)	Dry (D)	Mesic (M)	Wet (W)	INLAND Arid (A)	Dry (D)	Mesic (M)	Wet (W)	KAU'I	O'AHU	MOLOKA'I	LĀNA'I	MAUI	HAWAI'I	FULL SUN	PARTIAL SUN	SHADE	WELL DRAINED SOIL	IDEAL WATER (1-5*)	SALT TOLERANT
Alaheʻe	Psydrax odorata			D	M			D	M		X	X	X	X	X	X	○	◐		X	2-3	
Āulu	Rockia sandwicensis							D	M	W	X	X	X	X	X	X	○	◐		X	3-4	
Hala	Pandanus tectorius	↓	A	D	M	W		D	M	W	X	X	X	X	X	X	○			X	2-3	Y
Hala pepe	Dracaena aurea								M		X						○	◐		X	3	
Hala pepe	Dracaena auwahiensis							D	M				X		X		○			X	2-3	
Hala pepe	Dracaena forbesii							D	M			X					○	◐		X	2	
Hala pepe	Dracaena hawaiiensis							D	M							X	○	◐		X	2-3	
Hame	Antidesma pulvinatum							D	M			X	X	X	X	X	○	◐		X	3	
Hau	Hibiscus tiliaceus	↓	A	D	M	W			M	W	X	X	X	X	X	X	○	◐		X	2-4	Y
Hau hele ʻula	Kokia drynarioides	↓						D								X	○	◐		X	2	
Hōʻawa	Pittosporum confertiflorum								M	W		X		X	X	X	○	◐		X	2-3	
Hōʻawa	Pittosporum glabrum								M	W	X	X	X	X	X		○	◐		X	2-3	
Hōʻawa	Pittosporum hosmeri								M	W					X		○	◐		X	2-3	
Hōʻawa	Pittosporum napaliense								M		X						○	◐		X	2-3	
ʻIliahi	Santalum freycinetianum							D	M			X					○	◐		X	1-2	
Kamani	Calophyllum inophyllum	↓	A	D	M	W			M		X	X	X	X	X	X	○			X	1-2	Y
Kauila	Alphitonia ponderosa							D	M		X	X	X		X	X	○			X	2-3	
Kauila	Colubrina oppositifolia							D	M			X			X		○			X	1-2	
Kāwaʻu	Ilex anomala	↑							M	W	X	X	X	X	X	X	○	◐		X	4	

* 1. extremely drought tolerant (once established, would rarely need additional water); 2. accustomed to dry soils (in periods of drought, water 1-2/month once established); 3. accustomed to moist but tolerates occasionally dry; 4. prefers continuously moist soils; 5. wet to submerged (water feature)

Special status in red   Canoe in green

HEIGHT / WIDTH (feet)	ACCENT	CONTAINER: X CLIFF PLANT: C	GROUND COVER	HEDGE <5'	SCREEN >5'	SPECIMEN	TRELLIS/CLIMBER	SHADE COOLING	WATER FEATURE	FRAGRANT	COMMENTS (C)=challenging and for more experienced gardeners; (S)=short lived
10-30 / 10	X	X			X	X				X	Excellent tree with delightfully fragrant white flowers, and shiny green leaves. Reliably forms a narrow cone shape, but may grow as a shrub (and has been pruned for bonsai).
40-50 / 20	X	X			X	X		X		X	Attractive trees with slightly fragrant flowers. Sticky fruit was used to trap native birds and can be a nuisance near walkways.
10-32 / 20+	X	X			X	X		X		X	Lovely trees. Dioecious with male and female flowers on separate plants. Female trees have pineapple-shaped fruit. Male trees have fragrant flowers. Not drought-tolerant: arid where coastal and can access a fresh water lens. Note: it produces long, spiny leaves which need to be cleaned in an urban setting.
10-20 / 6-15	X	X				X					
5-20 / 3-15	X					X					Produces a beautiful display of greenish yellow tubular flowers and decorative red berries. *Dracaena forbesii* tends to be more shrub-like, but listed here so they're together. *Dracaena aurea* needs more moisture while others listed here are more drought-tolerant.
10-23 / 6-15	X	X			X	X		X			
16-20 / 10-15	X					X					
6.5-40 / 15-20	X				X	X		X			Attractive, easy to care for tree (or shrub) and excellent for privacy screening.
7-33 / 15+	X	X			X						Its soft wood was used for canoe outriggers, fishnet floats, and inner bark for cordage. Will spread and fill in quickly under the right conditions (cut tunnels through the dense thicket to add unique ambiance).
15-27 / 15						X					Maple-like leaves and stunning red to salmon flowers; relatively easy to grow and drought-tolerant after the first year (but may lose leaves during dry spells).
6.5-30 / 10-15	X				X	X				X	
13-26 / 10-15	X				X	X				X	Beautiful plants with lovely foliage and creamy white flowers that are especially fragrant at night. *Pittosporum confertiflorum* can grow as a shrub or a tree, the others are trees. All listed here are appropriate for mesic or wet conditions except *P. napaliense* which naturally occurs in just mesic areas.
10-26 / 10-15	X				X	X				X	
16-36 / 10-15	X				X	X				X	
3-42 / 10-20	X				X	X		X		X	This beautiful and easy to grow tree requires a host (koa or naio), but it's not considered picky. Its health depends on the health of the host plant (avoid spraying herbicides in the area). Does well in urban landscaped areas.
26-66 / 40						X		X		X	Valuable wood for canoes, for housing and carved into a wide range of everyday items. Has numerous medicinal properties and the flowers smell of orange blossoms. Note: drops many nuts.
15-40 / 10-30		X				X		X			Has one of the hardest woods of Hawaiian plants, and is a beautiful tree that should be more widely used.
16-43 / 10-28	X				X	X		X			Excellent for dry or mesic landscapes. Once established, avoid overwatering to prevent water shoots and a shrubbier appearance.
10-40 / 40	X				X			X			(C) Needs low light at lower elevations. Note: hard to find and best for experienced gardeners. Fruit prized by ʻōmaʻo or Hawaiian thrush.

Common Name	Scientific Name	prefers <2,000 ft / prefers >2,000 ft	C-Arid (A)	C-Dry (D)	C-Mesic (M)	C-Wet (W)	I-Arid (A)	I-Dry (D)	I-Mesic (M)	I-Wet (W)	KAU'I	O'AHU	MOLOKA'I	LĀNA'I	MAUI	HAWAI'I	FULL SUN	PARTIAL SUN	SHADE	WELL DRAINED SOIL	IDEAL WATER (1-5*)	SALT TOLERANT
Keahi	*Sideroxylon polynesicum*							D	M		X	X	X	X	X	X	○	◐		X	2	
Koa	*Acacia koa*	↑						D	M	W	X	X	X	X	X	X	○	◐		X	3	
Koai'a	*Acacia koaia*						A	D	M				X	X	X	X	○	◐		X	1-2	
Kōlea	*Myrsine lessertiana*								M	W	X	X	X	X	X	X	○	◐		X	3-4	
Kōpiko 'ula	*Psychotria hawaiiensis*								M	W			X		X	X		◐		X	3-4	
Kou	*Cordia subcordata*	↓	A	D	M	W					X	X	X	X	X	X	○	◐		X	1-2	Y
Kukui	*Aleurites moluccana*			D	M	W		D	M	W	X	X	X	X	X	X	○			X	2-4	Y
Lama	*Diospyros sandwicensis*							D	M	W	X	X	X	X	X	X	○	◐		X	1-2	
Lonomea	*Sapindus oahuensis*							D	M		X	X					○	◐		X	2-3	
Loulu	*Pritchardia beccariana*									W						X	○	◐		X	4	
Loulu	*Pritchardia glabrata*								M	W					X		○	◐		X	3-4	
Loulu	*Pritchardia hillebrandii*				M	W							X				○	◐		X	2-3	Y
Loulu	*Pritchardia maideniana* (Formerly *P. affinis*)	↓	A	D	M				M							X	○	◐		X	2	Y
Loulu	*Pritchardia martii*									W		X					○	◐		X	3-4	
Loulu	*Pritchardia remota*			D				D					Nihoa				○			X	1-2	Y
Mai'a (banana)	*Musa acuminata*								M	W	X	X	X	X	X	X	○	◐		X	3-4	
Māmane	*Sophora chrysophylla*	↑						D	M		X	X	X	X	X	X	○			X	1-2	
Manele, hawaiian soapberry	*Sapindus saponaria*	↑							M							X	○			X	2-3	
Manono	*Kadua affinis*								M	W	X	X	X	X	X	X		◐		X	3	

* 1. extremely drought tolerant (once established, would rarely need additional water); 2. accustomed to dry soils (in periods of drought, water 1-2/month once established); 3. accustomed to moist but tolerates occasionally dry; 4. prefers continuously moist soils; 5. wet to submerged (water feature)

Special status in red   Canoe in green

HEIGHT / WIDTH (feet)	ACCENT	CONTAINER: X CLIFF PLANT: C	GROUND COVER	HEDGE <5'	SCREEN >5'	SPECIMEN	TRELLIS/CLIMBER	SHADE COOLING	WATER FEATURE	FRAGRANT	COMMENTS (C)=challenging and for more experienced gardeners; (S)=short lived
6-33 / 25					X	X				X	These attractive small trees are easy to maintain and do well in urban landscapes.
15-60 / 20-40					X	X		X			(S) While they may be short-lived (5-20 yrs) in urban lowland settings, there is value in planting this amazing endemic tree to maintain connections with our forests. Ask for a koa inoculated with rhizobia.
15-30 / 20					X	X		X			Beautiful small tree with a straight trunk and round canopy. Closely related to *Acacia koa*, but does much better as a landscape plant at lower elevations.
6.5-40 / 4.3-26.4	X				X	X					Stunning plant but hard to find. Beautiful trees and shrubs with striking new leaves. Be careful when planting, it does not like root disturbance.
10-39 / 20					X	X					Requires a moist environment and prefers partial shade. Fruit prized by 'ōma'o or Hawaiian thrush. Wood was used for anvils and fuel.
15-50 / 30						X		X			Fast growing, low maintenance, moderately drought-tolerant and pest resistant. Note: tripping hazard from slippery fruits and exceptionally hard seeds. Tolerates some salt spray, but heavier spray will damage leaves.
32-65 / 50					X	X		X			A plant of many traditional uses, the oil from its nuts were used for lighting, the meat had many medicinal uses, and the bark was used for dyes. Note other plants may struggle to grow around it.
6.5-33 / 20	X				X	X		X			The colors of new growth (liko) include vibrant shades of red, magenta, pink or orange. Numerous early Hawaiian and modern uses.
20-50 / 40					X	X		X			Lovely, easy to grow tree. Very drought-tolerant once established.
52-63 / 12-15											This slow growing native palm makes a nice canopy, and over time can get quite tall.
3-7 / 10-12					X	X					A nice short-statured palm for a native landscape.
19-23 / 4-7						X					An attractive coastal plant that does well in a small grove in landscaped areas.
15-30 / 12-25						X					This native palm does well in hot dry leeward and urban coastal areas.
15-40 / 8-10	X					X					A small attractive palm that makes a nice addition to a residential planting.
13-17 / 10-12					X	X		X			This drought-tolerant and easy to maintain palm does well in dry hot urban areas. Faster growing than other loulus.
12-20 / 8	X				X						(S) An essential staple of Pacific cultures, every part was used. Listed here because it's tree-like, it's actually an herb and the stalk dies once it produces fruit, and then regenerates from new shoots.
6-50 / 3-20				X	X	X					This shrub or small tree does well in landscaped urban areas, but does not do well in a pot. Sometimes challenging to establish.
30-82 / 50						X		X			Beautiful trees that do well in urban landscapes. Large, so plan accordingly.
6-25 / 10	X	X		X	X	X					Decorative purple berries. Variable in form (shrub vs. tree) so inquire what form you're getting.

COMMON NAME	SCIENTIFIC NAME	↓ prefers <2,000 ft / ↑ prefers >2,000 ft	COASTAL				INLAND				KAU'I	O'AHU	MOLOKA'I	LĀNA'I	MAUI	HAWAI'I	FULL SUN	PARTIAL SUN	SHADE	WELL DRAINED SOIL	IDEAL WATER (1-5*)	SALT TOLERANT
			Arid (A)	Dry (D)	Mesic (M)	Wet (W)	Arid (A)	Dry (D)	Mesic (M)	Wet (W)												
Milo	*Thespesia populnea*	↓	A	D	M	W					X	X	X	X	X	X	○	◐		X	2-3	Y
Naio	*Myoporum sandwicense*		A	D			A	D	M	W	X	X	X	X	X	X	○			X	2	Y
Niu	*Cocos nucifera*		A	D	M	W					X	X	X	X	X	X	○			X	2-3	Y
Noni	*Morinda citrifolia*	↓	A	D	M	W	A	D	M	W	X	X	X	X	X	X	○	◐		X	1-3	Y
ʻOhe	*Polyscias hawaiensis (formerly Tetraplasandra)*								M	W		X	X	X	X	X	○	◐		X	2-3	
Ohe makai	*Polyscias sandwicensis (formerly Reynoldsia)*				M		A	D	M			X	X	X	X	X	○			X	1-2	
Ohiʻa ʻAi	*Syzygium malaccense*	↓							M	W	X	X	X	X	X	X	○	◐		X	2-3	
ʻŌhiʻa lehua	*Metrosideros polymorpha var. glaberrima*							D	M	W	X	X	X	X	X	X	○	◐		X	2-3	
ʻŌhiʻa lehua	*Metrosideros polymorpha var. incana*							D	M	W		X	X	X	X	X	○	◐		X	2-3	
ʻŌhiʻa lehua	*Metrosideros polymorpha var. polymorpha*							D	M	W		X	X	X	X	X	○	◐		X	2-3	
ʻŌlapa	*Cheriodendron trigynum*	↑							M	W	X	X	X	X	X	X		◐	●	X	3-4	
Olomea	*Perrottetia sandwicensis*								M	W	X	X	X	X	X	X		◐	●	X	3-4	
Olopua	*Nestegis sandwicensis*							D	M		X	X	X	X	X	X	○	◐		X	2-3	
Pāpala	*Charpentiera obovata*							D	M	W	X	X	X	X	X	X	○	◐		X	3-4	
Pāpala	*Charpentiera ovata var. niuensis*							D	M	W		X						◐		X	2-3	
Pāpala kēpau	*Ceodes brunoniana*								M	W		X	X	X	X	X	○	◐		X	3-4	
Pāpala kēpau	*Ceodes umbellifera*								M	W	X	X	X	X	X	X	○	◐		X	3-4	
Pilo, Hupilo	*Coprosma rhynchocarpa*	↑							M	W					X	X		◐		X	3	
Pōkalakala	*Polyscias racemosa (formerly Munroidendron)*			D	M			D	M		X						○			X	1-2	Y

TREE

* 1. extremely drought tolerant (once established, would rarely need additional water); 2. accustomed to dry soils (in periods of drought, water 1-2/month once established); 3. accustomed to moist but tolerates occasionally dry; 4. prefers continuously moist soils; 5. wet to submerged (water feature)

Special status in red   Canoe in green

HEIGHT / WIDTH (feet)	ACCENT	CONTAINER: X CLIFF PLANT: C	GROUND COVER	HEDGE <5'	SCREEN >5'	SPECIMEN	TRELLIS/CLIMBER	SHADE COOLING	WATER FEATURE	FRAGRANT	COMMENTS (C)=challenging and for more experienced gardeners; (S)=short lived
16-33 / 35						X		X			Forms a dense canopy for shade (and produces more litter than average). Beautiful wood carved into utensils, furnishings and jewelry. The bark is used for cordage and also has medicinal uses.
3.3-40 / 4.5-20	X	X	X	X	X					X	Lovely plant with a fast growth rate. May grow as a prostrate ground cover or upright tree depending on origin. At time of printing, not widely available to limit spread of an invasive thrips.
30-100 / 25	X					X					Provides food, drink, material for housing, cordage, clothing, and many other needs. Listed in arid and dry, but this is where it's at a low coastal elevation to access a fresh water lens.
10-20 / 15					X	X					Its fruit and juice is used medicinally for a number of ailments, and its fruit was a famine food for Native Hawaiians.
23-66 / 10-20						X		X			Beautiful and easy to grow. May be narrow and tall or shorter and broad depending on origin.
40-65 / 30-40		X				X					Lovely tree. Will drop its leaves in the dry season (but this typically reveals a beautiful branching pattern of limbs).
26-50 / 30						X		X			In addition to a source of food (mountain apple), its trunk was used for houses, and its bark and leaves for medicinal purposes.
6-60 / 4-25						X		X			'Ōhi'a lehua holds tremendous value ecologically and culturally. Stunning flowers may be red, yellow or orange and are prized by pollinators (especially honeycreepers at higher elevations). It has numerous recognized varieties, but those more commonly listed at nurseries are shown here. Select what occurs on your island and ask a nursery specialist to help you select a variety appropriate for your location. Most listed here may grow as shrubs or trees. See heights listed, but recognize there is wide variety and they are slow growing.
6-60 / 4-25						X		X			
6-40 / 4-15						X		X			
16-40 / 14-33	X										(C) Will do best in cooler, higher elevations. Do not plant the trunk too deep. Early Hawaiians valued it for bird catching, dye, hula, lei, medicinally and for weapons (spears).
6-20 / 10-15						X					(C) Attractive plants, but hard to find. Should do well in wet windward areas at lower elevations.
26-82 / 30	X				X	X		X			A lovely tree that should be grown more. Tolerates dry to mesic conditions.
13-20 / 8-13	X				X						Small red or yellow flowers are insignificant on their own, but showy en masse with the red stems. Tolerates full sun, but best in partial shade.
10-30 / 10	X	X			X						This understory plant does well in wet or moist conditions, and does well in a pot.
10-50 / 10-20	X				X	X		X		X	Attractive trees with slightly fragrant flowers. Sticky fruit was used to trap native birds and can be a nuisance near walkways.
10-33 / 20	X				X	X		X		X	
9-25 / 6-16.5	X										Great understory trees for 'ōhi'a and koa and red berries are prized by native birds.
15-33 / 15-20	X	X			X	X		X			Quick to flower and fruit and easy to grow. Has great potential for lowland and urban areas. Attractive and unique flowering structure.

	COMMON NAME	SCIENTIFIC NAME	prefers <2,000 ft (↓)	prefers >2,000 ft (↑)	COASTAL Arid (A)	Dry (D)	Mesic (M)	Wet (W)	INLAND Arid (A)	Dry (D)	Mesic (M)	Wet (W)	KAU'I	O'AHU	MOLOKA'I	LĀNA'I	MAUI	HAWAI'I	FULL SUN	PARTIAL SUN	SHADE	WELL DRAINED SOIL	IDEAL WATER (1–5*)	SALT TOLERANT
TREE	Uhiuhi	*Mezoneuron kavaiense*								D	M		X	X		X	X	X	○			X	1	
TREE	'Ulu	*Artocarpus altilis*	↓				M	W			M	W	X	X	X	X	X	X	○			X	2-3	
TREE	Wiliwili	*Erythrina sandwicensis*			A	D	M		A	D	M		X	X	X	X	X	X	○			X	1-2	Y
VINE	'Āwikiwiki	*Canavalia galeata*								D	M			X					○	◑		X	1-2	
VINE	'Āwikiwiki	*Canavalia hawaiiensis*								D	M					X	X	X	○	◑		X	1-3	
VINE	'Āwikiwiki	*Canavalia pubescens*			A	D	M		A	D	M		X			X	X		○	◑		X	2	
VINE	Bonamia	*Bonamia menziesii*								D	M	W	X	X	X	X	X	X	○	◑		X	1-2	
VINE	Huehue	*Coccolus orbiculatus*			A	D	M	W	A	D	M	W	X	X	X	X	X	X	○	◑		X	2	Y
VINE	Hunakai	*Ipomoea imperati*	↓		A	D							X	X	X		X		○			X	1-2	Y
VINE	Ipu	*Lageneria siceraria and vulgaris*	↓		A	D	M	W			M	W	X	X	X	X	X	X	○			X	2	
VINE	Maile	*Alyxia stellata*								D	M	W	X	X	X	X	X	X	○	◑		X	2-3	
VINE	Nanea	*Vigna marina*	↓		A	D	M	W					X	X	X		X	X	○	◑		X	1-2	Y
VINE	Nanea	*Vigna o-wahuensis*							A	D	M			X	X	X	X	X	○	◑		X	1-2	
VINE	Pā'ū o Hi'iaka	*Jacquemontia sandwicensis*	↓		A	D			A	D			X	X	X	X	X	X	○			X	1-2	Y
VINE	Pōhuehue	*Ipomoea pes-caprae* subsp. *brasiliensis*	↓		A	D	M	W					X	X	X	X	X	X	○			X	1-2	Y
VINE	'Uala	*Ipomoea batatas*				D	M			D	M		X	X	X	X	X	X	○	◑		X	3	
VINE	Uhi	*Dioscorea alata*	↓		A	D	M	W			M	W	X	X	X	X	X	X	○	◑		X	2	

* 1. extremely drought tolerant (once established, would rarely need additional water); 2. accustomed to dry soils (in periods of drought, water 1-2/month once established); 3. accustomed to moist but tolerates occasionally dry; 4. prefers continuously moist soils; 5. wet to submerged (water feature)

Special status in red   Canoe in green

HEIGHT / WIDTH (feet)	ACCENT	CONTAINER: X CLIFF PLANT: C	GROUND COVER	HEDGE <5'	SCREEN >5'	SPECIMEN	TRELLIS/CLIMBER	SHADE COOLING	WATER FEATURE	FRAGRANT	COMMENTS (C)=challenging and for more experienced gardeners; (S)=short lived
13-33 / 8-21					X	X					(C) Plant when young to prevent from becoming root bound. Monitor for twig borers. Water regularly to help establish, but then only during drought (too much water will reduce flowering).
40-70 / 30-50						X		X			Stunning tree for large spaces and a major food source for Native Hawaiians. The fruit is becoming a more valued crop.
35-45 / 30-40						X		X			These stately trees drop their leaves to conserve water (usually during summer), then put on a stunning display of orange to salmon colored flowers before leafing out again. Fixes nitrogen. Extremely drought-tolerant once established.
0.2-0.4 / 10+	X	X	X				X				
0.2-0.4 / 10+	X	X	X				X				Produces beautiful pea shaped flowers, generally purple but may also be pink with a white spot near base. Great groundcover over cinder or rocks, or to cover a trellis or fence.
0.2-0.4 / 10+	X	X	X				X				
5-10 / 15+	X						X	X			Long-lived vine is excellent for chain link fences or trellises, and flowers are in almost constant bloom.
1-2 / 3-5	X		X				X				Sprawling long-lived, partially woody vine could be a filler, or a sparse ground cover.
0.2-0.3 / 15+	X		X								Easy-to-grow plant needs room to spread and looks spectacular over coral rocks or sand.
0.75-1.5 / 15+	X	X	X				X				This useful gourd can store water, serve as a syringe, pot, and rattle and drum to accompany the hula.
2-5.5 / 6-10	X	X	X				X			X	Sprawling partially woody vine with a fragrant flower, does well as an accent plant or in the understory. Some forms are great for a trellis.
0.2-0.4 / 10+	X		X				X				Lovely, fast growing groundcover with yellow flowers for coastal sites.
0.2-0.3 / 0.3-1.3	X	X	X				X				Charming plant with beautiful yellow flowers.
0.25-0.75 / 10+	X		X								Looks stunning spilling over rock walls, in hanging baskets or as a groundcover. Blueish white flowers are 1" wide. Denser varieties in development for hanging baskets.
0.2-0.3 / 15+			X								Great vine with decorative flowers to fill in an area. Usually coastal but should do ok mauka given adequate drainage and full sun.
0.3-0.6 / 15+	X	X	X								Produces nutritious tubers and leaves, and has many medicinal uses.
0.3-1 / 10+											The Hawaiian yam was a traditional food source grown throughout the islands.

Chapter Four

This chapter provides designs for three common landscape scenarios: a lanai, walkway and yard—for each of the eight climates zones shown in the maps of Chapter 2 and the Quick Reference Table of Chapter 3. These designs probably won't look exactly like your property, but we hope that the suggested combinations and their layouts help you to design and plant a community that is diverse, visually harmonious and, by working in layers and minimizing bare ground, requires less maintenance. Please note: this section provides brief summaries for the plants featured. See the Quick Reference Table for more detailed information on these plants or to find substitutes.

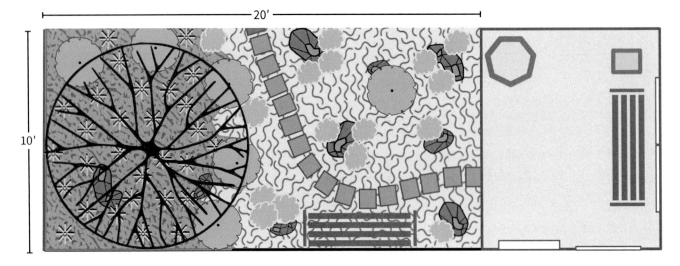

'Iliahialo'e (Santalum ellipticum) is a large shrub to small tree and would look beautiful in this more intimate, coastal arid setting. Determine the origin of the plant you acquire as coastal 'iliahialo'e are low to medium shrubs, and inland plants tend to be trees. 'Iliahialo'e is drought-tolerant, relatively pest resistant and new leaves and flowers can be an attractive reddish color. They are not difficult to grow, but are hemi-parasitic, meaning they require a host plant. Their root system penetrates the roots of some nearby host plants and they depend on the health of these neighboring plants for their survival so it's critical to avoid the use of herbicides in their vicinity. They are described as not being picky about the identity of the host plant, and 'akoko (below) should work well. **Spacing:** allow a 10' canopy. **Alternatives:** 'A'ali'i (Dodonaea viscosa).

'Akoko (Euphorbia celastroides var. celastroides) is in the same family as poinsettia and this lovely plant can serve as an accent, specimen or hedge. The bluish leaf color provides a nice color contrast. Plants do best in full sun and are drought and wind tolerant once established. The milky sap of 'akoko was used as a supplement for lactating mothers, for weaning a child, and mixed with poi for infants (however, please note that sap from Euphorbia is an eye irritant). **Spacing:** 5'. **Alternatives:** dwarf naupaka (Scaevola coriacea), naupaka kuahiwi (Scaevola gaudichaudii). Naupaka kahakai (Scaevola taccada) could also be used but is pretty large for this space and would need to be trimmed back routinely.

Ma'oli'oli (Schiedea globosa) is easy to grow and looks great in pots or hanging baskets. While individual flowers are not showy, their form is showy *en masse*. It naturally occurs on steep, rocky slopes or cliffs in coastal habitats, often north-facing, meaning this plant can do well in partial shade. The genus *Schiedea* is in the Caryophyllaceae family, also known as the Pink family, including catchflies, pinks and carnations. **Spacing:** 1-2'

DAVID EICKHOFF

Mau'u 'aki'aki *(Fimbristylis cymosa)* is attractive as an accent, groundcover or in pots. Use well-drained soil and if in a pot, remove the saucer so water doesn't pool. It looks great in rock gardens and is an excellent drought-tolerant alternative to mondo grass. While it prefers full sun, it will tolerate partial shade. **Spacing:** for understory and perimeter of 'iliahialo'e, plant 6" apart and ensure 3-5 are within 1-2' of 'iliahialo'e.

'Ōhelo kai *(Lycium sandwicense)* naturally occurs among rocks along the coast and is well adapted to salt spray and high heat. The narrow succulent leaves are pale green. It has small white to blue-tinted flowers and produces small red berries (the berries are not poisonous, but not particularly tasty). It's naturally a leggy, sprawling shrub, but regular trimming will encourage side branches and a denser growth. Be mindful that this plant is adapted to very dry conditions, and, once established, it will not do well if overwatered. **Spacing:** 1-2' Alternative: 'ōhai *(Sesbania tomentosa)*.

'Ihi *(Portulaca lutea)* is a succulent, drought-tolerant plant that does well as an accent, groundcover or in pots. There are numerous native Hawaiian species of 'ihi or Portulaca with *P. lutea* being more prostrate. It's recommended to let it spill over the edge in pots.

For a larger pot (2'+ diameter), we recommend a combination of 'ihi, 'ōhelo kai (see above) and mau'u 'aki'aki (see above). Space 'ihi roughly 12" apart at the perimeter of the pot to spill over the edge. The focal point plant is 'ōhelo kai, and mau'u 'aki'aki is used as a filler spaced 6" apart. Well-drained soil (no deep saucer allowing water to pool) is essential for all these plants.

Nehe *(Lipochaeta integrifolia* [formerly *Melanthera integrifolia])* should be used more often given its bright flowers that bloom year round. This plant is well adapted to coastal sites with salt spray, wind and high heat. However, it does need regular water until established and showing signs of new growth (then taper off or plants get scraggly). When watering, try to water the ground rather than the foliage (to reduce disease). This plant is great between tall stepping stones in low-traffic areas, as a filler, or spilling over retaining walls. Trim to increase denser branching and trim heavily once a year to encourage new growth. **Spacing:** plant 1' apart for quick coverage, or 2-3' if you're patient (but this will require more weeding as weeds love open ground).

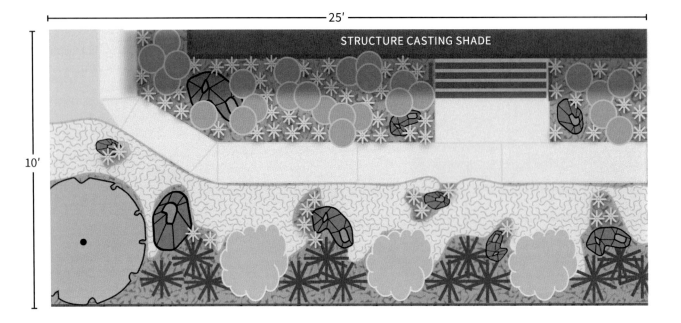

25'

10'

STRUCTURE CASTING SHADE

Ma'o *(Gossypium tomentosum)* has lovely bright yellow flowers, and the silvery green, palmate or 3-5 lobed leaves add a nice feature to the landscape. The yellow flowers were used to make a green dye (ma'o is the Hawaiian word for green). This plant does best when left to grow naturally versus as a formal hedge, but some pruning is helpful to keep it bushy. It needs no additional water once established (and will suffer with automatic irrigation). It forms a decorative cotton mass after flowering and has been used to breed pest resistant traits into commercial cotton.
Spacing: 4-5'

'Ala'ala wai nui *(Peperomia blanda var. floribunda, P. mauiensis, P. sandwicensis, P. tetraphylla)* are great as accents or in pots in partially shady locations. Of the numerous native Hawaiian *Peperomia* species, *Peperomia blanda* var. *floribunda* would be best for this setting as it's considered the most drought-tolerant. This design has it planted in informal clusters intermixed with the drought-tolerant mau'u 'aki'aki (see below). Alena (*Boerhavia repens*) is a third species to consider, but place it along the edge of the pathway in the full sun areas. **Spacing: 1' Alternatives:** drought-tolerant species for shade are not common, but 'āweoweo (*Chenopodium oahuense*) is an option for larger spaces. It prefers full sun, but will tolerate partial shade.

Mauʻu ʻakiʻaki *(Fimbristylis cymosa)* is an attractive plant as an accent, and groundcover. It looks great in rock gardens and is an excellent drought-tolerant alternative to mondo grass. While it prefers full sun, it will tolerate partial shade as featured in this setting. **Spacing:** 6"

Pili *(Heteropogon contortus)* is a tough, drought-tolerant grass and makes a great accent plant. While drought-tolerant, it will have a greener, more vibrant look with some additional moisture. Along with serving as an accent, it can be a groundcover when planted more densely. There are more upright and prostrate forms available. **Spacing:** 1-2.5'

Nehe *(Lipochaeta integrifolia [formerly Melanthera integrifolia])* should be used more often given its bright flowers that bloom year round. This plant is tolerant of harsh conditions in coastal areas including salt spray, wind and high heat. However, it does need regular watering until it's established and showing signs of new growth (then taper off or plants get scraggly). When watering, try to water the ground rather than the foliage (to reduce disease). This plant is great between tall stepping stones in low traffic areas, as a filler, or spilling over retaining walls. **Spacing:** 0.75-2' (planting farther apart initially saves money, but will require more weeding while plants fill in).

ʻAhinahina *(Achyranthes splendens* var. *rotundata)* has silvery gray foliage and a nice growth form, as well as decorative silvery seed heads. It's easy to grow and is quick to flower and produce seed (and will spread by seed). This plant is federally endangered (there are scattered populations on the ʻEwa Plains and at Kaʻena Point on Oʻahu). **Spacing:** 4'

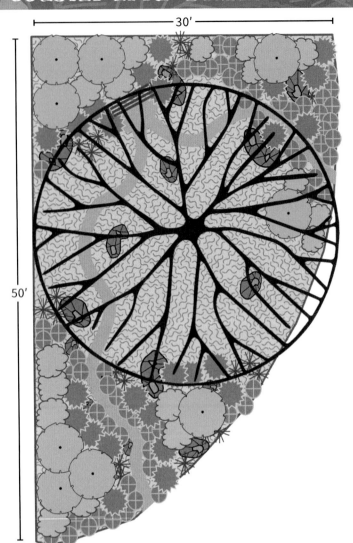

30'

50'

Wiliwili (Erythrina sandwicensis) is a beautiful and unique tree as a specimen or planted *en masse* in larger areas. They drop their leaves to conserve water, then put on a stunning display of orange flowers before leafing out again. They fix nitrogen and are extremely drought-tolerant once established. Seed pods twist open (wiliwili means "twist-twist") to expose brightly colored seeds which are valued for making lei. **Spacing:** allow a 40' width. Note: Some species that are not shade tolerant are shown in the understory of the wiliwili (like 'ohai, ma'o). These are recommended to provide some form and suppress weeds while the wilwili canopy develops and then they may fade out. **Alternatives:** Kou *(Cordia subcordata)* for those wanting shade year round.

Pili (Heteropogon contortus) is a tough, drought-tolerant grass and makes a great accent plant. While drought-tolerant, it will have a greener, more vibrant look with some additional moisture. Along with serving as an accent, it can be a groundcover when planted more densely. There are more upright and prostrate forms available. **Spacing:** 1.5-2'

Hinahina (Heliotropium anomalum var. argenteum) means "silvery" in the Hawaiian language, an apt name for this attractive groundcover, which looks particularly stunning over rocks. Although adapted to harsh, dry coastal environments, it needs more regular watering in landscaped areas until established. It must have full sun. In this design, it's in the understory in some areas, but this is to provide some cover for weed suppression until the canopy develops and then it may fade out. Its flowers and leaves are valued for lei. **Spacing:** 6-12"

Dwarf Naupaka (*Scaevola coriacea*) is an endangered, but easy to grow coastal plant that's great for full sun, windy, dry conditions with salt spray. It has small fragrant flowers and makes an attractive groundcover or accent plant over rocks. It needs little water once established. **Spacing:** 2-3' (note-this species is very slow growing, so 2' recommended unless you're very patient). **Alternatives:** 'Ilima papa (*Sida fallax*) for some color (could also consider 'akoko (*Euphorbia degeneri*) or 'ihi (*Portulaca molokiniensis*).

'Ohai (*Sesbania tomentosa*) is variable in size, growing as a low shrub or a small tree. The smaller form, 2-3' tall, is what is most commonly available at most nurseries, and intended for this particular design, but please ask about the source of the plant as taller, more upright forms are now becoming more widely available. Both forms have silvery green leaves and spectacular flowers which make any landscaped area sparkle. It does particularly well as an accent, and needs full sun and little water once established. **Spacing:** 2-4'

'Ilie'e (*Plumbago zeylanica*) is a great ground cover, especially useful for stabilizing soil to reduce erosion (and it's also unpalatable to goats). Use in place of wedelia and non-native plumbagos. Plants withstand heavy pruning and this helps keep them contained and encourages dense branching. It can be grown as a low hedge, or a more natural rambling shrub for larger areas as shown here. While it prefers full sun, it will tolerate partial shade better than many other plants suitable to arid conditions. Note: Seeds heads are sticky and spread easily on shoes, clothing, and animal fur. **Spacing:** 2'

Ma'o (*Gossypium tomentosum*) has lovely bright yellow flowers, and the silvery green, palmate or 3-5 lobed leaves add a nice feature to the landscape. The yellow flowers were used to make a green dye (ma'o is the Hawaiian word for green). This plant does best when left to grow naturally versus as a formal hedge, but some pruning is helpful to keep it bushy. It needs no additional water once established (and will suffer with automatic irrigation). It forms a decorative cotton mass after flowering and has been used to breed pest-resistant traits into commercial cotton. **Spacing:** 3-4'

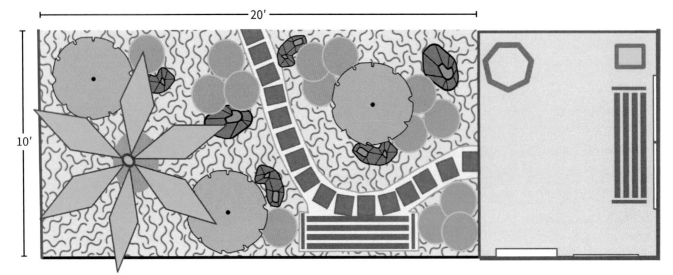

‹20'›

10'

Loulu (*Pritchardia remota*), endemic to the island of Ni'ihau, is one of 19 different species of Loulu native to Hawai'i. It's drought-tolerant, easy to maintain and does well in hot, dry urban areas. It is similar to other species of *Pritchardia*, especially *P. hillebrandii*, but is usually faster growing, has a thinner leaf texture, drooping leaf segments that are more deeply divided and smaller fruit. **Spacing:** allow an 8-10' canopy. **Alternatives:** *Pritchardia maideniana* (formerly *P. affinis*) would also do great here being adapted to arid and dry zones (but a bit larger, so not as ideal if space is really limited).

'Ilima papa (*Sida fallax*) is a lovely plant with flower color spanning the yellow to orange spectrum and some forms with a dark red base. Note there is 'ilima and 'ilima papa and 'ilima papa is what is recommended here. 'Ilima is typically from higher elevations, taller in stature and less drought-tolerant. 'Ilima papa is a shorter, more drought-tolerant form from the lowlands, with size and water needs appropriate for this design and climate. Heavy watering (like from an automated sprinkler system) will cause fungal rot or black sooty mold, and plants will decline rapidly. This plant is the island flower of O'ahu and prized for making lei 'ilima. **Spacing:** 20-24"

Maiapilo (*Capparis sandwichiana*) is a small- to medium-sized sprawling shrub with beautiful, fragrant flowers. The flowers are night-blooming and last just one day. This is a great plant for xeriscaping as it requires very little water once established. **Spacing:** 3-5'

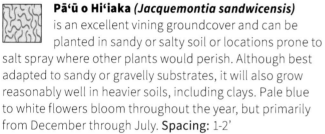

Pāʻū o Hiʻiaka *(Jacquemontia sandwicensis)* is an excellent vining groundcover and can be planted in sandy or salty soil or locations prone to salt spray where other plants would perish. Although best adapted to sandy or gravelly substrates, it will also grow reasonably well in heavier soils, including clays. Pale blue to white flowers bloom throughout the year, but primarily from December through July. **Spacing:** 1-2'

ʻAkoko *(Euphorbia degeneri)* is a sprawling, low growing shrub with beautiful medium green leaves that have a reddish tinge. It's great as an accent, ground cover and in pots. Note the milky sap of *Euphorbia* is an eye irritant and can cause skin irritation. For larger pots, consider including mauʻu ʻakiʻaki *(Fimbristylis cymosa)* which is seen growing in the background in the photo. **Spacing:** 1-2' **Alternatives:** Maʻoliʻoli *(Schiedea globosa)* or Oahu Sedge *(Carex wahuensis).*

MOʻOLELO

Pāʻū o Hiʻiaka translates to skirt of Hiʻiaka. According to the story, Pele was out on the water and left her baby sister Hiʻiaka on the beach. She was gone longer than expected and Hiʻiaka fell asleep. A vine grew up and covered her like a skirt to protect her from the sun - hence Pāʻū o Hiʻiaka. Besides the beauty of the white to pale blue flowers, an extra benefit of growing this plant is that it's a pollen and nectar source for an endangered native yellow-faced bees (*Hylaeus* spp).

Pōkalakala *(Polyscias racemosa [formerly Munroidendron racemosum])* is a small tree endemic to Kauaʻi. It's rare in the wild as its native habitat, coastal dry and mesic forest, has been largely destroyed. Small yellow flowers hang in long, pendulous rope-like strands. It's sparingly branched and can lose most of its leaves during the summer, but this reveals an attractive branching structure. Its unique flowering structure and status as an endangered plant make it a great conversation piece as a potted plant on your lanai. **Alternatives:** ʻaʻaliʻi *(Dodonaea viscosa)* or ʻākia *(Wikstroemia uva-ursi).*

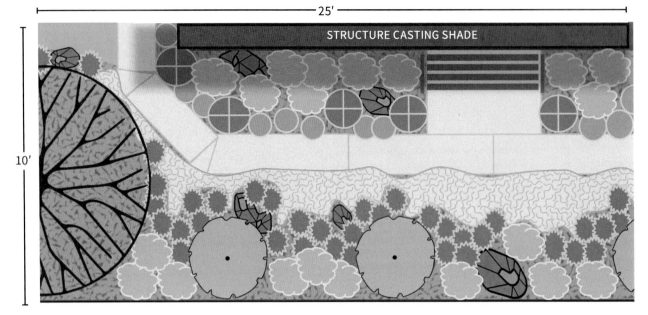

25'

10'

STRUCTURE CASTING SHADE

'Ākia (Wikstroemia uva-ursi) is typically a low, sprawling shrub with orange-red berries. It responds well to pruning and can easily be shaped into a denser, more compact form. It does well in xeriscaped landscaping and looks spectacular flowing over rocks or low walls. The flowers and decorative fruit are used for making lei haku. 'Ākia was used as a poison to stun fish, making them easy to catch. **Spacing:** 2-3' (in this design, they are spaced farther than 3' for a more natural look, but they may be spaced 2' on center for a denser, continuous form).

Alahe'e (Psydrax odorata) has earned the nickname the Christmas tree plant thanks to the showy white flowers that appear to light up its uniform cone shape. Leaves are bright green and glossy. Plants are drought-tolerant, but do well in moist conditions as long as the soil is well-drained. **Spacing:** allow a 10' width.

'Ala'ala wai nui wahine (Plectranthus parviflorus) is a spreading, herbaceous, low-growing plant whose native habitat is dry exposed and often rocky locations. It does best in partial sun, but tolerates a range of exposures from sun to shade. Decorative fuzzy leaves are fleshy and have scalloped edges and the plant produces small, light blue flowers. This plant may be short lived, but will regenerate from seed and pop up in new places (meaning it will fill in empty spaces in place of weeds). **Spacing:** 1'

'Ōhelo kai (*Lycium sandwicense*) naturally occurs among rocks along the coast and is well adapted to salt spray and high heat. The narrow succulent leaves are pale green. It has small white- to blue-tinted flowers and produces small red berries (the berries are not poisonous, but not particularly tasty). It's naturally a leggy, sprawling shrub, but regular trimming will encourage side branches and a denser growth. Be mindful that this plant is adapted to very dry conditions and once established, it will not do well if overwatered. It's difficult to find native Hawaiian plants adapted to dry conditions that also do well in shade. While this plant prefers full sun, it will tolerate partial shade. **Spacing:** 1-2'

Hinahina (*Heliotropium anomalum* var. *argenteum*) means "silvery" in the Hawaiian language, an apt name for this attractive groundcover, which looks particularly stunning over rocks. Although adapted to harsh, dry coastal environments, it needs more regular watering in landscaped areas until established. It must have full sun. Its flowers and leaves are valued for lei. **Spacing:** 6-12"

Ma'oli'oli (*Schiedea globosa*) is easy to grow and looks great in pots or hanging baskets. While individual flowers are not showy, their form is showy *en masse*. It naturally occurs on steep, rocky slopes or cliffs in coastal habitats, often on north-facing locations, meaning this plant can do well in partial shade. The genus *Schiedea* is in the Caryophyllaceae family, also known as the Pink family, including catchflies, pinks and carnations.

Pā'ū o Hi'iaka (*Jacquemontia sandwicensis*) is an excellent vining groundcover and can be planted in sandy or salty soil or locations prone to salt spray where other plants would perish. Although best adapted to sandy or gravelly substrates, it will also grow reasonably well in heavier soils, including clays. Pinch to create a denser branching pattern. Pale blue to white flowers bloom throughout the year, but primarily from December to July. **Spacing:** 1-2'

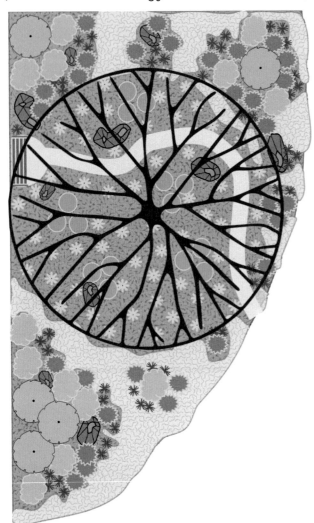

30'

50'

Kou (Cordia subcordata) is an excellent, easy to grow tree with decorative orange flowers. It grows quickly, but does have a shallow root system which can be damaged by surface disturbance. It prefers full sun and needs little water once established. It tolerates saline soils and some salt spray, but heavier spray will damage leaves. The wood was traditionally prized for carving and was also used for fish hooks. Be careful about planting this around sidewalks as the slippery fruit and hard seeds can pose a tripping hazard. **Spacing:** allow a 30' canopy.

Maiapilo (Capparis sandwichiana) is a small to medium sprawling shrub with beautiful flowers. The fragrant flowers are night-blooming and last just one day. This is a great plant for xeriscaping, as it requires very little water once established. **Spacing:** 4-5'

Oʻahu sedge (Carex wahuensis subsp. wahuensis) is a graceful sedge that forms thick clumps. In a garden it is attractive as an accent, around the base of taller plants or as a border. It prefers partial sun and needs little water once established. The leaves and seed clusters can be used in lei or in floral arrangements. Typical of most sedges, it does have sharp/abrasive leaf edges. **Spacing:** 1.5-2'

Pili (Heteropogon contortus) is a tough, drought-tolerant grass and makes a great accent plant. While drought-tolerant, it will have a greener, more vibrant look with some additional moisture. Along with serving as an accent, it can be a groundcover when planted more densely. There are more upright and prostrate forms available. **Spacing:** 1.5-2'

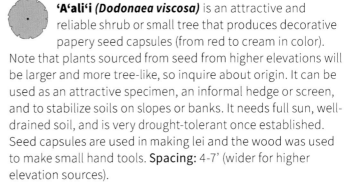

'A'ali'i *(Dodonaea viscosa)* is an attractive and reliable shrub or small tree that produces decorative papery seed capsules (from red to cream in color). Note that plants sourced from seed from higher elevations will be larger and more tree-like, so inquire about origin. It can be used as an attractive specimen, an informal hedge or screen, and to stabilize soils on slopes or banks. It needs full sun, well-drained soil, and is very drought-tolerant once established. Seed capsules are used in making lei and the wood was used to make small hand tools. **Spacing:** 4-7' (wider for higher elevation sources).

Kō'oko'olau *(Bidens menziesii* **subsp.** *filiformis* **or subsp.** *menziesii)* has attractive yellow flowers and does well as an accent plant or even as a hedge. While it prefers full sun, it is used in this design to provide some structure, color, and weed reduction while the tree canopy develops. Once the canopy fills in, it will fade out (and the tree's shade should greatly reduce time spent weeding). **Spacing:** 3-4' **Alternatives:** Moa *(Psilotum nudum)* is a fern-like plant that adds a unique form to the garden and would do well in the partial shade here.

'Ākia *(Wikstroemia uva-ursi)* is a low, sprawling shrub with orange-red berries. It responds well to pruning and can easily be shaped into a denser, more compact form. It does well in xeriscaped landscaping and looks spectacular flowing over rocks or low walls. The flowers and decorative fruit are used for making lei haku. 'Ākia was used as a poison to stun fish, making them easy to catch. **Spacing:** 2-3'

'Ākulikuli *(Sesuvium portulacastrum)* makes a nice ground cover for coastal settings and is well adapted to the harsh, dry conditions and salt spray there. It forms a dense mat and has succulent leaves and attractive pink flowers. Allow it to dry between waterings. The flowers, leaves and branches are used for lei. **Spacing:** 6-12" **Alternatives:** Pā'ū o Hi'iaka *(Jacquemontia sandwicensis)*, nehe *(Lipochaeta integrifolia)*. Alena *(Boerhavia repens)* could be included as well, not as the primary ground cover, but for more ground cover diversity.

coastal mesic LANAI

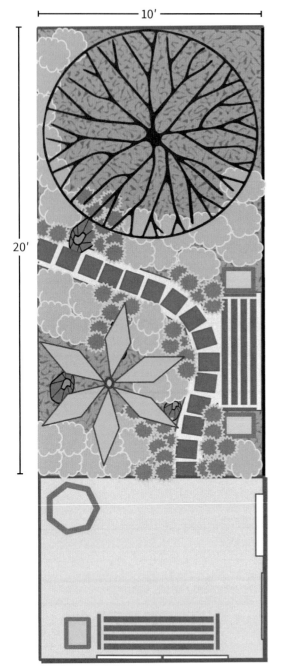

10'

20'

The current layout shows a more naturalized design with pockets of 'uki 'uki amidst large swaths of pōhinahina. If you want a more formal look, you could space the shorter form of 'uki 'uki in dense clusters in front of the pōhinahina at systematic intervals along the pathway.

Alahe'e (Psydrax odorata) has earned the nickname the Christmas tree plant thanks to the showy white flowers that appear to light it up when it's in bloom. It also has a uniform cone-shaped profile like a Christmas tree, making it a nice specimen for this intimate setting. It's generally low maintenance, the white flowers are fragrant and it has bright green, glossy leaves. It is drought-tolerant, but does well in moist conditions as long as the soil is well-drained. **Spacing: 10'**

Loulu (Pritchardia hillebrandii) is a small, attractive fan palm. While slow growing, it's easy to grow given full sun and good drainage. It does well in low elevation sites and tolerates salt spray. It looks great in small groups of three or more, or can be grown as a specimen as shown here. This species is at risk, formerly common along the northern coast of Moloka'i, but extinct there today (likely due to goats and rats). **Spacing: allow a 7' width. Alternatives:** *Pritchardia maideniana* (formerly *P. affinis*) is an option if the space is wider (it tends to be broader than *P. hillebrandii*); for smaller spaces, a group of ki (*Cordyline fruticosa*) would create a nice vertical accent.

Pōhinahina *(Vitex rotundifolia)* is an amazing low-growing shrub and a workhorse, especially in tough urban environments where it can be seen thriving in narrow commercial strips or sidewalk medians. Plants produce showy light purple flowers. Leaves also emit a nice fragrance, almost sage-like. This is a dependable plant that is especially suited for the novice gardener. It responds well to pruning and will need periodic pruning as it will extend into the walkway. Spacing: 2-3'

'Uki'uki *(Dianella sandwicensis)* is a great accent plant with delicately beautiful flowers. There's a short compact form (1-1.5' tall) with brilliant bluish-purple fruits; a taller, thinner-leafed one (3') with brownish-purple fruits; and a white-fruited form with paler green leaves. It naturally occurs in somewhat open to shaded sites usually in mesic forests (but also in dry shrubland, grassland on lava and in wet forests). In this design, it's recommended in the understory of the loulu and as an accent, placed periodically along the pathway, but the pōhinahina will need to be more vigilantly trimmed to not overwhelm it. It also looks great and does well in containers. **Spacing:** 1-2'

Ālula *(Brighamia insignis)* are fairly easy to grow in pots in a partly sunny location, but MUST have a well-aerated soil mix (i.e., for succulents and cactus, or mixes containing black cinder) for perfect drainage and they do need frequent watering. If growing in the ground, again ensure excellent drainage (consider adding black cinder) in a partly sunny location and protect from slugs and snails. Flowers produce a sweet smell similar to honeysuckle or citrus. This plant is federally endangered.

Manono *(Kadua littoralis)* are partially woody, shrub-like plants bearing bright white flowers and beautiful glossy leaves. They naturally occur on wet rocky sea cliffs and rocky coastal areas, meaning they are great in well-drained pots and containers and are tolerant of salt spray. This at risk plant is now extinct on Oʻahu (but still found at Princeville, Kauaʻi; from Hālawa to Wailau valleys, Molokaʻi; Keʻanae-Wailua area, Hanawī, and ʻĀlau, East Maui; Honopue, Hawaiʻi). **Spacing:** 1'
Alternatives: 'uki'uki *(Dianella sandwicensis)*.

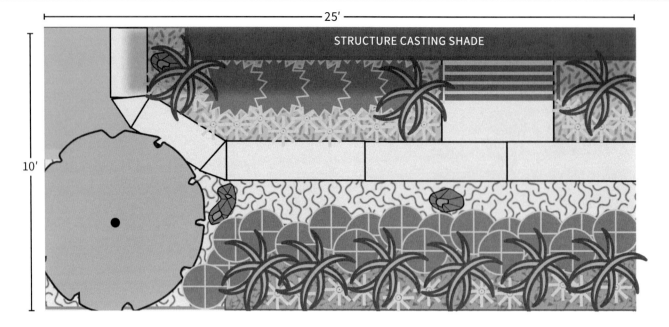

25'

10'

STRUCTURE CASTING SHADE

Hame (Antidesma pulvinatum) is a small hardwood tree native to the dry to mesic forests and wet zones along the coast. It is not common, but if you can find it, it makes a great addition to the landscape. Hame's attractive glossy foliage is dark maroon when young and dark green when older. Its wood was used to make anvils for beating kapa, and its berries made a dye. **Spacing:** allow 10-15' **Alternatives:** canoe plants such as mai'a (banana, *Musa acuminata*), 'ohe (bamboo, *Schizostachyum glaucifolium*), kō (sugarcane, *Saccharum officinarum*).

Ki (Cordyline fruticosa) is a canoe plant with leaves used for thatch, food wrappers, hula skirts, and sandals. Plants do well in full sun or partial shade, and benefit from protection from the wind. Many varieties are available with various leaf colors, but the original Polynesian introduction was green. **Spacing:** 3-4'

FOREST & KIM STARR

'Ihi'ihi (Marsilea villosa) is a unique fern with leaves like 4-leaf clovers. While it's endangered, it's relatively easy to grow, and spreads rapidly with periodic moisture. It's not essential to this design, but the showy leaves are a nice feature, and it will fill in empty spaces, reducing the need to weed. Although it's adapted to ephemeral wetlands or areas that are seasonally wet and then dry, it does not require this for survival (at UH Mānoa it's thriving at a native plant garden that gets some supplemental irrigation, but is never wet like an ephemeral [seasonal] pool). Watering may restore growth if it dries out. Spacing: 1'

unless otherwise noted, all photos by David Eickhoff

O'ahu sedge *(Carex wahuensis* subsp. *wahuensis)* is a graceful sedge that forms thick clumps. In a garden it is attractive as an accent, around the base of taller plants or as a border. It needs full or partial sun and little water. The leaves and seed clusters can be used in lei or in floral arrangements. Typical of most sedges, it does have sharp/abrasive leaf edges. **Spacing: 1.5-2'**

'Ilima papa *(Sida fallax)* is a lovely plant with flower color spanning the yellow to orange spectrum and some forms with a dark red base. Note there is 'ilima and 'ilima papa and the lower growing 'ilima papa is recommended here. 'Ilima is typically from higher elevations, taller in stature and less drought-tolerant. 'Ilima papa is a shorter, more drought-tolerant form from the lowlands. Heavy watering (like from an automated sprinkler system) will cause fungal rot or black sooty mold, and plants will decline rapidly. This plant is the island flower of O'ahu and prized for making lei 'ilima. **Spacing: 20-24"**

'Awapuhi *(Zingiber zerumbet)* has stunning flowers and grows well in partial to even full shade. While slow-growing, like most gingers it will creep out and can take over if not managed. It dies back annually so best not to feature it as the specimen in a design. The O'ahu sedge suggested in the foreground will provide some cover and interest while it's dormant. Traditionally, and at present, this plant is used in shampoos, both directly and processed (check your shampoo bottle!) **Spacing: 3-4'**

Pā'ū o Hi'iaka *(Jacquemontia sandwicensis)* is an excellent vining groundcover and can be planted in sandy or salty soil or locations prone to salt spray where other plants would perish. Although best adapted to sandy or gravelly substrates, it will also grow reasonably well in heavier soils, including clays. Pinch to create a denser branching pattern. Pale blue to white flowers bloom throughout the year, but primarily from December to July. **Spacing: 1-2' Alternatives:** Nanea *(Vigna marina)* or for a canoe plant theme, 'uala *(Ipomoea batatas)* makes a rambling ground cover, produces beautiful flowers, and the sweet potatoes can be harvested yearly.

coastal mesic 59

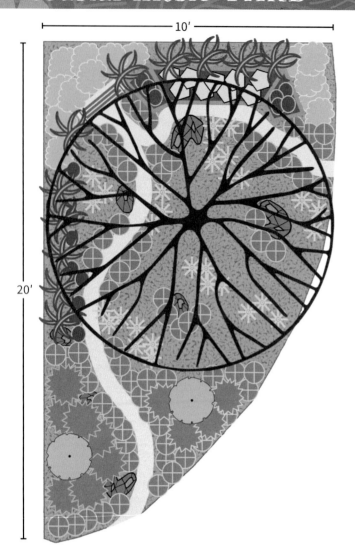

10'

20'

'Ulu (Artocarpus altilis) is a beautiful tree that forms a dense canopy with striking leaves. The starchy fruit is a key food source in many parts of the Pacific. As the Hawai'i 'Ulu Cooperative notes, it sequesters and stores carbon while it grows and feeds us! While adapted to low elevation coastal areas, it's not suitable for sites with direct salt spray. **Spacing:** allow a 30-40' canopy (this is a large tree needing plenty of space). **Alternatives:** Kou (Cordia subcordata), kukui (Aleurites moluccana), or milo (Thespesia populnea).

'Akia (Wikstroemia oahuensis) is a large shrub or small tree which does well as a specimen and has a lovely night fragrance similar to jasmine. The bark was traditionally used to make strong cordage, and the plant also has medicinal uses. **Spacing:** 5' **Alternatives:** Alahe'e (Psydrax odorata).

'Ūlei (Osteomeles anthyllidifolia) (shrub) is a hardy and versatile shrub with fragrant white flowers. It's naturally sprawling but can be pruned to make it more compact. It needs full sun and well-drained soil. **Spacing:** 3'

Naupaka kahakai (Scaevola taccada) is a dependable beach shrub which also does well inland. It makes a good windbreak or hedge and is easy to grow from cuttings. It needs full sun and little water once established and has small, but attractive white flowers. **Spacing:** 2-3' for a dense hedge.

Ki *(Cordyline fruticosa)* is a Polynesian introduction with leaves used for thatch, food wrappers, hula skirts, and sandals. Plants do well in full sun or partial shade, and benefit from protection from the wind. Many varieties are available with various leaf colors, but the original Polynesian introduction was green. **Spacing:** 3-4'

'Uki'uki *(Dianella sandwicensis)* is a great accent plant with delicately beautiful flowers. There's a short compact form (1-1.5' tall) with brilliant bluish-purple fruits; a taller, thinner leafed one (3') with brownish-purple fruits; and a white-fruited form with paler green leaves. It occurs naturally in somewhat open to shaded sites usually in mesic forests. **Spacing:** 1-2'

Kalo *(Colocasia esculenta)*, a canoe plant with many varieties, is perhaps the most important plant in Hawaiian culture. All parts of the plant except the stem are eaten. All varieties are ornamental and make attractive specimens and planted together make a nice lo`i (taro patch)! See the Resource Guide for more information on growing this plant.

'Olena *(Curcuma longa)* has gorgeous flowers and roots have medicinal and culinary value (this is turmeric, prized as an anti-inflammatory). Plant rhizomes 4" deep. Note that plants will die back and go dormant during the winter. **Spacing:** 1.5'

O'ahu sedge *(Carex wahuensis* **subsp.** *wahuensis)* is a graceful sedge that forms thick clumps. In a garden it is attractive as an accent, around the base of taller plants or as a border. It needs full or partial sun and little water. The leaves and seed clusters can be used in lei or in floral arrangements. Typical of most sedges, it does have sharp leaf edges. **Spacing:** 1.5-2'

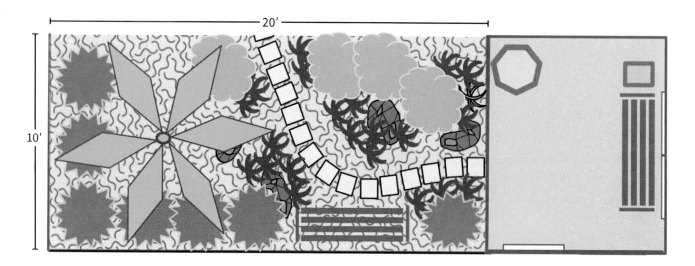

20'

10'

Loulu *(Pritchardia hillebrandii)* is a small, attractive fan palm. While slow growing, it's easy to grow given full sun and good drainage. It does well at low-elevation sites and tolerates salt spray. It looks great in small groups of three or more, or can be grown as a specimen as shown here. This species is at risk, formerly common along the northern coast of Moloka'i, but extinct there today (likely due to goats and rats). **Spacing:** allow a 7' width. **Alternatives:** for larger site, hala *(Pandanus tectorius)*.

'Ilima *(Sida fallax)* has beautiful flowers that may be bright yellow, orangish yellow, light orange, rich orange, or rusty red (and some with dark red at the base). There are two forms, 'ilima and 'ilima papa. 'Ilima is the more upright form that is typically less drought-tolerant and what is recommended for this design. 'Ilima papa is a lower growing form from lower elevations that is more drought-tolerant. This plant is the island flower of O'ahu and prized for making lei 'ilima. **Spacing:** 3-4'

Ki *(Cordyline fruticosa)* is a Polynesian introduction with leaves used for thatch, food wrappers, hula skirts, and sandals. Plants do well in full sun or partial shade, and benefit from protection from the wind. Many varieties are available with various leaf colors, but the original Polynesian introduction was green. **Spacing:** 3-4'

DAVID EICKHOFF

DAVID EICKHOFF

Neke *(Cyclosorus interruptus)* is a very attractive fern, about 2' tall, with beautiful fronds prized for making lei. An experienced native plant specialist believes this plant is underrepresented and under-valued in the landscape industry and should be used more widely given its beauty. It will do well in this wet coastal design as it naturally occurs along the sides of streams and in marshy areas. It also does well in containers and is suggested for the smaller container in this design. **Spacing:** 1.5'. **Alternatives:** Ama'u *(Sadleria cyatheoides)* is another stunning fern, but is much larger (requiring a 4-5' spacing). Palapalai *(Microlepia strigosa* var. *strigosa)* is not listed in the coastal zones, but can do fine in sites more sheltered from salt spray.

Nanea *(Vigna marina)* is a great vine for coastal sites as it is highly tolerant of salty soils and windy conditions. It produces yellow flowers and fixes nitrogen, providing other plants in the area with a source of fertilizer. It does need regular trimming to confine it to where it's planted or it will scramble up taller plants (and will do well on a trellis). This plant is edible; seeds can be cooked like other dry peas. **Spacing:** 1-3' **Alternatives:** Ae'ae *(Bacopa monnieri)* is a less aggressive option for smaller spaces, and it would do well between stepping stones.

Ae'ae *(Bacopa monnieri)* is a fairly dense, short ground cover with light green leaves and blueish white flowers. Its natural habitat is mud flats, sand, rocks, marshes, and brackish stream shores. It will form a dense cover with consistent moisture. It's recommended in this design around the base of kalo in the larger container. It has numerous medicinal benefits (as an anti-inflammatory and for memory enhancement). **Spacing:** 1-3'

Kalo *(Colocasia esculenta)*, a canoe plant with many varieties, is perhaps the most important plant in Hawaiian culture. All parts of the plant except the stem are eaten. All varieties are ornamental and make attractive specimens, and planted together make a nice lo'i (taro patch)! See the Resource Guide for information on growing this plant.

STRUCTURE CASTING SHADE

10'

25'

Loulu (Pritchardia hillebrandii) is a small, attractive fan palm. While slow-growing, it's easy to grow in full sun and with good drainage. It does well in low-elevation sites and tolerates salt spray. **Spacing: 7' Alternatives:** 'Ohe (bamboo, *Schizostachyum glaucifolium*) or for larger spaces with a 15-20' width: coconut (*Cocos nucifera*) or noni (*Morinda citrifolia*).

'Uki'uki (Dianella sandwicensis) is a great accent plant with delicately beautiful flowers. There's a short compact form (1-1.5' tall) with brilliant bluish-purple fruits; a taller, thinner-leafed one (3') with brownish-purple fruits; and a white-fruited form with paler green leaves. It naturally occurs in somewhat open to shaded sites usually in mesic forests (but ranges from dry shrubland to wet forest). Spacing: 1-2'

Ki (Cordyline fruticosa) is a canoe plant with leaves used for thatch, food wrappers, hula skirts, and sandals. Plants do well in full sun or partial shade, and benefit from protection from the wind. Many varieties are available with various leaf colors, but the original Polynesian introduction was green. **Spacing: 3-4'**

DAVID EICKHOFF

DAVID EICKHOFF

Kalo *(Colocasia esculenta)*, a canoe plant with many varieties, is perhaps the most important plant in Hawaiian culture. All parts of the plant except the stem are eaten. All varieties are ornamental and make attractive accents or specimens. See the Resource Guide for more information on growing this plant.

Ae'ae *(Bacopa monnieri)* is a fairly dense, short ground cover with light green leaves and bluish-white flowers. Its natural habitat is mud flats, sand, rocks, marshes, and brackish stream shores. It will form a dense cover with consistent moisture. It has numerous medicinal benefits (as an anti-inflammatory and for memory enhancement). **Spacing:** 1-3'

> Kalo, a food source essential to Hawaiian livelihood and culture, has numerous health benefits. High in fiber, it's great for gut health, managing body weight and blood sugar levels, and improving heart health. It also has high levels of potassium, magnesium, and vitamins C and E.

'Ahu'awa *(Cyperus javanicus)* is a greenish blue rush with umbrella-like flower clusters with small spikelets containing the seeds. It likes full sun and moist growing conditions. The color of the leaves makes a nice contrast with rock features. Note: sedges do have edges on the blade and can be abrasive or cause small cuts so it's not advised for heavily trafficked areas. **Spacing:** 1-1.5'

Neke *(Cyclosorus interruptus)* is a very attractive fern, about 2' tall, with beautiful fronds prized for making lei. An experienced native plant specialist and grower believes this plant is underrepresented and under-valued in the landscape industry and should be used more widely given its beauty. It will do well in this design for a wet zone as it naturally occurs along the margins of streams and in marshy areas. **Spacing:** 1.5'

DAVID EICKHOFF

├── 50' ──┤

30'

Naupaka kahakai *(Scaevola taccada,* [formerly *Scaevola sericea])* is a dependable beach shrub which also does well inland. It makes a good windbreak or hedge and is easy to grow from cuttings. It needs full sun and has small, but attractive white flowers. **Spacing:** 3-8' (closer if you want an immediate hedge).

Neke *(Cyclosorus interruptus)* is a very attractive fern, with lovely fronds prized for making lei. It should be used more widely given its beauty. **Spacing:** 1.5' **Alternatives:** 'Ahu'awa *(Cyperus javanicus)* with its blue-green foliage could be used in place of or in addition to neke.

Niu *(Cocos nucifera)* is a canoe plant providing humans the essentials of food, drink, oil, medicine, fiber, timber, thatch, mats and fuel. Plants must have full sun. **Spacing:** 15-25'. Dwarf varieties are available for home gardens that produce smaller nuts earlier (3 vs 5 yrs) and more prolifically. Their short stature makes the coconuts easier to harvest. The "niu leka" dwarf from Fiji, also known as the "Samoan Dwarf" in Hawai'i produces short stiff fronds and large nuts.

Hala *(Pandanus tectorius)* is a hardy and visually striking plant that does well as a specimen with its unusual growth form or in a grove as shown here. Male and female flowers are on separate plants and female plants have pineapple-shaped fruit and male plants have fragrant flowers. Leaves are used for hats, jewelry and other items, and its fruit is used in lei. **Spacing:** allow a 15-25' width.

DAVID EICKHOFF

Manono _(Kadua littoralis)_ is a partially woody, shrub-like plant bearing bright white flowers and beautiful glossy leaves. It occurs naturally on wet rocky sea cliffs and coastal talus. This at-risk plant is now extinct on Oʻahu (but still found on Princeville, Kauaʻi; from Hālawa to Wailau valleys, Molokaʻi; Keʻanae-Wailua area, Hanawī, and ʻĀlau, East Maui; Honopue, Hawaiʻi). **Spacing:** 1' **Alternatives:** ʻUkiʻuki _(Dianella sandwicensis)_, Kōʻokoʻolau _(Bidens hillebrandiana)_.

FOREST & KIM STARR

Kalo _(Colocasia esculenta)_, a canoe plant, is one of the most important plants in Hawaiian culture. All parts of the plant except the stem are eaten. There are wetland and dryland varieties available (it's believed that early Hawaiians developed more than 150 cultivars of kalo). See the Resource Guide for information on growing it. In addition to kalo, that strip could be subdivided to include ʻolena _(Curcuma longa)_, a beautiful medicinal plant (the source of turmeric), and ipu _(Lageneria siceraria,_ or _L. vulgaris),_ which produce useful, decorative gourds.

FOREST & KIM STARR

Pōhuehue _(Ipomoea pes-caprae)_ is an attractive and easy to maintain ground cover for dry areas, but also adapted to wet zones. The beautiful flowers add nice color to the landscape. **Spacing:** 2-4' **Alternatives:** This is a rambling vine. For denser coverage, consider nanea _(Vigna marina)_ and for smaller areas, aeʻae _(Bacopa monnieri)_ or ʻākulikuli _(Sesuvium portulacastrum)._

MOʻOLELO

Many stories exist as to why naupaka flowers appear split in half, but most center around forbidden love between two lovers of different rank: a princess and a commoner. In resignation, the princess tore a naupaka flower from her ear in half, giving one half to her lover who she sent back to the coast while she stayed in the mountains. The naupaka kuahiwi (mountain naupaka) and the naupaka kahakai (beach naupaka) saw their sadness and have only bloomed as half flowers ever since.

FOREST & KIM STARR

FOREST & KIM STARR

ʻAwapuhi _(Zingiber zerumbet)_ is a canoe plant with stunning flowers that grows well in partial to even full shade. While slow-growing, like most gingers it will creep out and can take over if not managed. It dies back annually so best not to feature it as the specimen in a design. **Spacing:** 3-4'

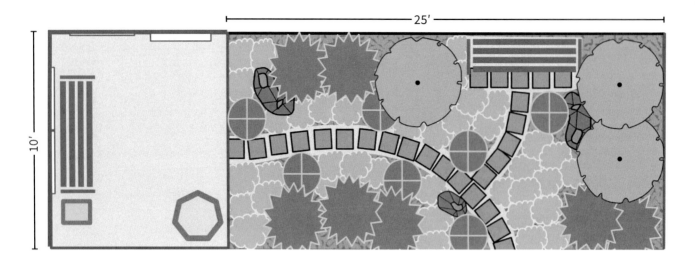

25'

10'

'A'ali'i *(Dodonaea viscosa)* is an attractive and reliable shrub or small tree that produces decorative papery seed capsules (from red to cream in color). Note that plants sourced from seed from higher elevations will be larger and more tree-like, so inquire about origin. 'A'ali'i can be used as an attractive specimen, an informal hedge or screen, and to stabilize soils on slopes or banks. It needs full sun, well-drained soil, and is very drought tolerant once established. Seed capsules are used in making lei and the wood was used to make small hand tools. **Spacing:** 4-7' **Alternatives:** A less common shrub that would also work well in this design is ko'oloa 'ula (*Abutilon menziesii*).

'Ilima papa *(Sida fallax)* is the low-growing, drought-tolerant form of 'ilima from lower elevations, distinct from the taller form from higher elevations that typically requires more water. Flower color varies and includes bright yellow, orangish yellow, light orange, rich orange, dull or rusty red, and some forms with dark red at the base. Heavy watering (like from an automated sprinkler system) will cause fungal rot or black sooty mold and plants will decline rapidly. This plant is the island flower of O'ahu and prized for making lei 'ilima. **Spacing:** 1.75-2.5' (to not clutter up the plot map, most are featured in singles, but it will look better as accents if planted in dense clusters of 2-3).

Maʻo hau hele *(Hibiscus brackenridgei)* is a beautiful hibiscus and the state flower of Hawaiʻi. The common name means "green traveling hau," referring to how this sprawling plant may topple over, root at the nodes, and form a new plant. When planted in the ground, periodic pruning will prevent this. In this design, you'll be reminded to do this periodic pruning to keep the plant from extending too far beyond the confines of the pot. There are three subspecies of maʻo hau hele listed in the quick reference guide that shows their presence by island. This plant is sometimes prone to rose beetles which cause holes in the leaves. Leaving lights on from dusk to 8 or 9 pm can reduce their presence. **Spacing:** 3-6'

Naupaka kuahiwi *(Scaevola gaudichaudii)* is one of only two naupakas with yellow flowers. The narrow petals are striking and they have a lovely fragrance. This plant naturally occurs on dry ridges and flats in open shrubland and forests. **Spacing:** 4' **Alternatives:** ʻĀweoweo *(Chenopodium oahuense)*, or maiapilo *(Capparis sandwichiana)*.

Pōhinahina *(Vitex rotundifolia)* is an amazing low-growing shrub and a workhorse, especially in tough urban environments where it can be seen thriving in narrow commercial strips or sidewalk medians. Pōhinahina also does well as a container plant. It produces showy, light purple flowers and the leaves also emit a nice fragrance, almost sage-like. This is a dependable plant that is especially suited to the novice gardener. It responds well to pruning (and will need more regular pruning in a design like this where it's next to a narrow walkway). **Spacing:** 2-3' in the ground; plant a bit closer to create a denser look more quickly in a pot.

Mauʻu ʻakiʻaki *(Fimbristylis cymosa)* is an attractive plant as an accent, groundcover or in pots (be sure to use well-drained soil and remove saucer so water doesn't pool). It looks great in rock gardens and is an excellent drought-tolerant alternative to mondo grass. While it prefers full sun, it will tolerate partial shade. **Spacing:** 6"

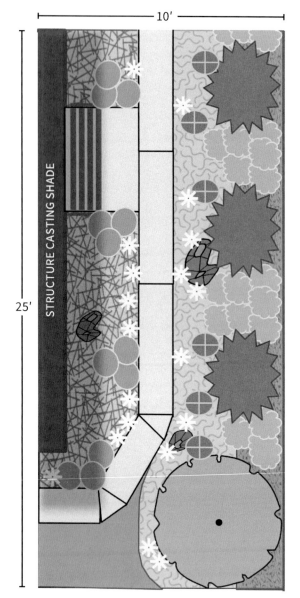

STRUCTURE CASTING SHADE

10'

25'

Koʻoloa ʻula (Abutilon menziesii) is a drought-tolerant shrub with spectacular red flowers. It can be used as a specimen and also works well as a hedge. It is naturally somewhat scraggly but can be pruned into a denser, more attractive shape. **Spacing:** 3-4'

Pōhinahina (Vitex rotundifolia) is an amazing low-growing shrub and a workhorse, especially in tough urban environments where it can be seen thriving in narrow commercial strips or sidewalk medians. Plants produce showy light purple flowers. Leaves also emit a nice fragrance, almost sage-like. It's a dependable plant especially suited to the novice gardener. **Spacing:** 2-3'

Mauʻu ʻakiʻaki (Fimbristylis cymosa) is an attractive plant as an accent, groundcover or in pots (with well-drained soil). It looks great in rock gardens and is an excellent drought-tolerant alternative to mondo grass. While it prefers full sun, it will tolerate partial shade. Alena *(Boerhavia repens)* is another species to include with mauʻu akiʻaki along the edge to fill in gaps and provide some color. **Spacing:** 6" minimum, but spaced wider here as accents.

ʻAlaʻala wai nui wahine (Plectranthus parviflorus) is a spreading, herbaceous, low-growing plant whose native habitat is dry exposed and often rocky locations. Decorative fuzzy leaves are fleshy and have scalloped edges. The plant produces small, light blue flowers. This plant may be short-lived, but will regenerate from seed and pop up in new places (meaning it will fill in empty spaces in place of weeds). **Spacing:** 1'

DAVID EICKHOFF

DAVID EICKHOFF

Pua kala *(Argemone glauca)*, or Hawaiian poppy has attractive white flowers, and the silvery, almost blue foliage makes a striking addition to the landscape. Pua kala, means "thorny flower," and it is one of a very few native plants that has prickles on the leaves and stems. It is easy to grow, somewhat short-lived, but will regenerate from seed (meaning it's best in a natural rather than formal design). This plant needs good drainage and little water. **Spacing:** 1.5-2'

'Ilie'e *(Plumbago zeylanica)* is a great ground cover, especially useful for stabilizing soil to reduce erosion. Use in place of wedelia and non-native plumbagos. Plants withstand heavy pruning and this helps keep them contained and encourages dense branching. Can be grown as a low hedge, or a more natural rambling shrub for larger areas. While it prefers full sun, it will tolerate partial shade as shown here. **Spacing:** 2'

Pā'ū o Hi'iaka *(Jacquemontia sandwicensis)* is an excellent vining groundcover. Although best adapted to sandy or gravelly substrates, it will also grow reasonably well in heavier soils, including clays. Pinch to create a denser branching pattern. Pale blue to white pā'ūohi'iaka flowers bloom throughout the year, but primarily from December to July. **Spacing:** 1-2'

Kulu'ī *(Nototrichium sandwicense)* is an attractive shrub with silvery green leaves that can be easily pruned and shaped for denser growth. It likes full sun and is easy to grow and maintain. Its flower spikes and leaves look good in head lei or floral arrangements. **Spacing:** 3'

inland arid   71

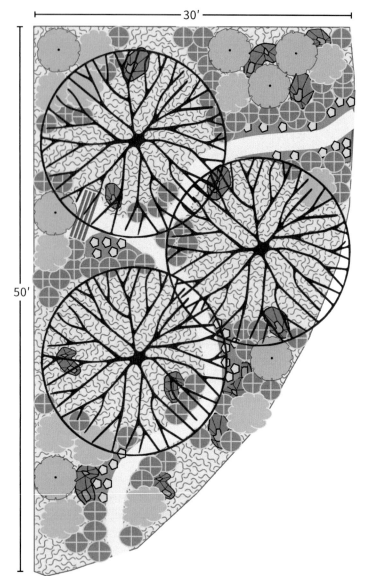

├── 30' ──┤

50'

DAVID EICKHOFF

DAVID EICKHOFF

Koaiʻa (Acacia koaia) is a small tree related to koa, adapted to dry conditions and needing full sun. It's a beautiful option for smaller landscapes or can be planted in groups in larger spaces. The wood is hard and dense and was used for kapa anvils, spears and fish hooks. **Spacing:** Allow a 15' width **Alternatives:** Wiliwili *(Erythrina sandwicensis)* is a magnificent tree and very drought-tolerant once established (see photos and summary in the coastal arid yard design).

Some of the more iconic flowers in Hawaii are those of Hibiscus, a member of the Malvaceae family. All plants in this family have funnel-shaped flowers with 5 separate petals and a prominent column of stamens surrounding the pistil. If you examine the stunning flowers of koʻoloa ʻula, or ʻilima papa, you'll see the same pattern - they're also members of the Malvaceae family. See if you can recognize a plant in the Malvaceae family in the coastal arid yard design (hint, the common name means green).

Koʻoloa ʻula (Abutilon menziesii) is a drought-tolerant shrub with spectacular red flowers. It can be used as a specimen and also works well as a hedge. It is naturally somewhat scraggly but can be pruned into a denser, more attractive shape. **Spacing:** 4' **Alternatives:** Maʻo hau hele *(Hibiscus brackenridgei)* produces beautiful flowers (see photos in inland arid lanai design) and could be used in place of a few or all the koʻoloa ʻula.

'**Ilima papa** (*Sida fallax*) is the low-growing, drought-tolerant form of 'ilima from lower elevations, distinct from the taller form from higher elevations that typically requires more water. Flower color varies and includes bright yellow, orangish yellow, light orange, rich orange, dull or rusty red, and some forms with dark red at the base. Heavy watering (like from an automated sprinkler system) will cause fungal rot or black sooty mold and plants will decline rapidly. This plant is the island flower of O'ahu and prized for making lei 'ilima. **Spacing:** 1.75-2.5' **Alternatives:** not as an alternative, but in place of a few clusters of 'ilima papa consider pua kala (*Argemone glauca*, see inland arid lanai for photos).

Maiapilo (*Capparis sandwichiana*) is a small to medium sprawling shrub with beautiful flowers. The fragrant flowers are night-blooming and last just one day. This is a great plant for xeriscaping as it requires very little water once established. **Spacing:** 4-5'

'**Ilie'e** (*Plumbago zeylanica*) is a great ground cover, especially useful for stabilizing soil to reduce erosion (and it's also unpalatable to goats). Use in place of wedelia and non-native plumbagos. Plants withstand heavy pruning and this helps keep them contained and encourages dense branching. It can be grown as a low hedge, or a more naturalized rambling shrub for larger areas as shown here. While it prefers full sun, it will tolerate partial shade better than many other plants suitable to arid conditions. **Spacing:** 2'-3'

'**Ihi** (*Portulaca molokiniensis* or *villosa*) are succulent, drought-tolerant plants requiring well-drained soil and full sun. *Portulaca molokiniensis* (far right) is more upright, with leaves that are stacked and *P. lutea* (right) is more prostrate. **Spacing:** 1-2' **Alternatives:** Additional low-growing, drought-tolerant plants for trailside interest are mau'u 'aki'aki (*Fimbristylis cymosa*), alena (*Boerhavia repens*) or nanea (*Vigna o-wahuensis*).

inland arid 73

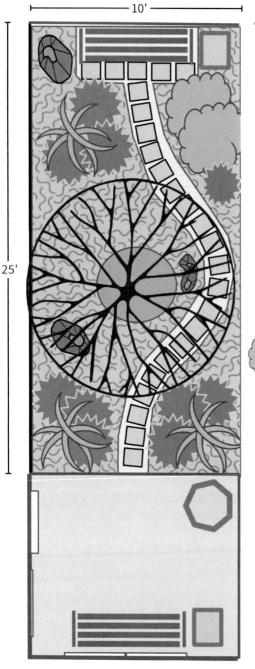

├── 10' ──┤

25'

Hala pepe (*Dracaena auwahiensis, D. forbesii,* or *D. hawaiiensis*) may be slow growing, but they are worth the effort. They are a great alternative to money tree (*Dracaena marginata*) and other non-native dracaenas. They produce beautiful displays of greenish yellow tubular flowers and decorative red berries. *Dracaena forbesii* tends to be more shrub-like. *Dracaena aurea* is adapted to a mesic rather than dry zone so not recommended here. **Spacing:** 4-6'

Kuluʻī (*Nototrichium sandwicense*) is an attractive shrub with silvery green leaves that can be easily pruned and shaped for denser growth (see photos of trimmed and untrimmed plants). It likes full sun and is easy to grow and maintain. Its flower spikes and leaves look good in head lei or floral arrangements. **Spacing:** 3'

Hau hele ʻula (*Kokia drynarioides*) is a striking native member of the hibiscus family. It has beautiful salmon-colored flowers and maple-like leaves. Its flower petals and bark were traditionally used to make dyes, and the bark also had medicinal uses. Its native habitat is dryland forest so its water needs are minimal once established. Sadly, it's critically endangered with just a couple of wild plants remaining on the big island of Hawaiʻi. **Spacing:** allow a 15' width **Alternatives:** if your space is indeed as narrow as that shown here, Kokia might be a bit too large, and it also can be hard to find. An ʻŌhiʻa lehua (*Metrosideros polymorpha*) or a cluster of nāʻū (*Gardenia brighamii*) would also work well here.

'Ākia *(Wikstroemia uva-ursi)* is a low sprawling shrub with orange-red berries. It responds well to pruning and can easily be shaped into a denser, more compact form. It does well in xeriscaped landscaping and looks spectacular flowing over rocks or low walls. The flowers and decorative fruit are used for making lei haku. 'Ākia was used as a poison to stun fish, making them easy to catch. **Spacing:** 2-3'.

Nā'ū *(Gardenia brighamii)* is a native gardenia that is rare in the wild but does well in gardens. Its attractive shape and flowers ask to be shown off, so plant it where it can be seen, but be patient as this plant is slow growing. The pulp from its seeds was used to make rich yellow dye and its wood was used to make house posts for people of high status. Its fragrant flowers make a beautiful lei. This plant is endangered. **Spacing:** Allow a 4' width in a pot.

Bonamia *(Bonamia menziesii)* is a long-lived vine that is excellent for chain link fences or trellises. Its flowers are in almost constant bloom. It's intended in this design to be up against a wall or fence with a trellis. This plant is endangered. **Alternatives:** If a trellis is not appropriate for your site, 'ala'ala wai nui *(Peperomia blanda var. floribunda)* is easy to grow and looks great in pots.

'Ilie'e *(Plumbago zeylanica)* is a great ground cover, especially useful for stabilizing soil to reduce erosion. Use in place of wedelia and non-native plumbagos. Plants withstand heavy pruning and this helps keep them contained and encourages dense branching. Can be grown as a low hedge, or a more naturalized rambling shrub for larger areas. **Spacing:** 2'

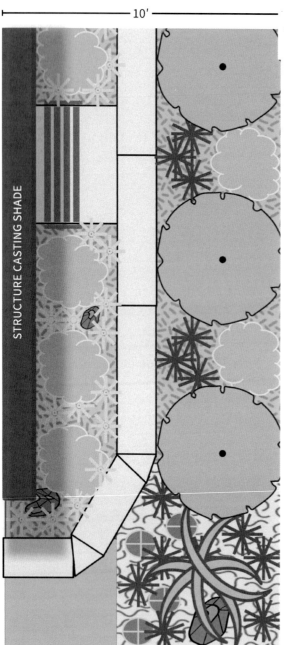

Hala pepe (*Dracaena auwahiensis, D. forbesii,* or *D. hawaiiensis*) may be slow-growing, but it is worth the effort. Hala pepe is a great alternative to money tree and other non-native dracenas. It produces beautiful displays of greenish yellow tubular flowers and decorative red berries. *Dracena forbesii* tends to be more shrub-like. *Dracena aurea* is adapted to a mesic rather than dry zone, so not recommended here. **Spacing:** Allow a 4' width.

Nāʻū (*Gardenia brighamii*) is a native gardenia that is critically endangered, but does well in cultivation. Its attractive shape and flowers ask to be shown off, so plant it where it can be seen, but be patient as this plant is slow growing. The pulp from its seeds was used to make rich yellow dye and its wood was used to make house posts for people of high status. Its fragrant flowers make a beautiful lei. **Spacing:** Allow a 6' width **Alternatives:** ʻAʻaliʻi (*Dodonaea viscosa*).

ʻIhiʻihi (*Marsilea villosa*) is a unique fern with leaves like 4-leaf clovers. While it's endangered, it's relatively easy to grow, and spreads rapidly with periodic moisture. It's not essential to this design, but the showy leaves are a nice feature, and it will fill in empty spaces (reducing the need to weed). Although it's adapted to ephemeral wetlands or areas that are seasonally wet and then dry, it does not require this for survival (at UH Mānoa it's thriving at a native plant garden that gets some supplemental irrigation, but is never wet like an ephemeral [seasonal] pool). Watering may restore growth if it dries out. Spacing: 1'

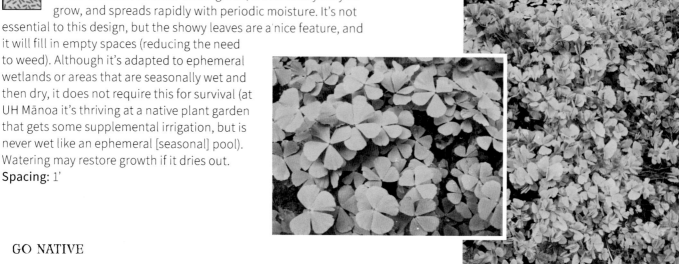

Pua kala *(Argemone glauca)* or Hawaiian poppy offers attractive white flowers and silvery gray foliage that make a striking addition to the landscape. It is one of the few native Hawaiian plants that has prickles and spines on its leaves and stems. It is easy to grow and somewhat short lived, but will regenerate from seed meaning it's best in a more natural rather formal design. This plant requires good drainage and needs little water. **Spacing:** 1.5' minimum

Kōʻokoʻolau *(Bidens menziesii* subsp. *filiformis* or subsp. *menziesii)* has attractive yellow flowers and does well as an accent plant or even as a hedge. While it prefers full sun, it will tolerate some shade. The leaves of kōʻokoʻolau are used to make tea. **Spacing:** 3-4'

Oʻahu sedge *(Carex wahuensis* subsp. *wahuensis)* is a graceful sedge that forms thick clumps. In a garden it is attractive as an accent, around the base of taller plants or as a border. It needs full or partial sun and little water. The leaves and seed clusters can be used in lei or in floral arrangements. Typical of most sedges, it does have sharp/abrasive leaf edges. **Spacing:** 1.5-2'

Pāʻū o Hiʻiaka *(Jacquemontia sandwicensis)* is an excellent vining groundcover. Although adapted to sandy or gravelly substrates, it will also grow reasonably well in heavier soils, including clays. Pinch to create a denser branching pattern. Pale blue to white flowers bloom throughout the year, but primarily from December to July. **Spacing:** 1-2'

Pili *(Heteropogon contortus)* is a tough, drought-tolerant grass and makes a great accent plant. While drought tolerant, it will have a greener, more vibrant look with some additional moisture. Along with serving as an accent, it can be a groundcover when planted more densely. There are more upright and prostrate forms available. **Spacing:** 1-2.5'

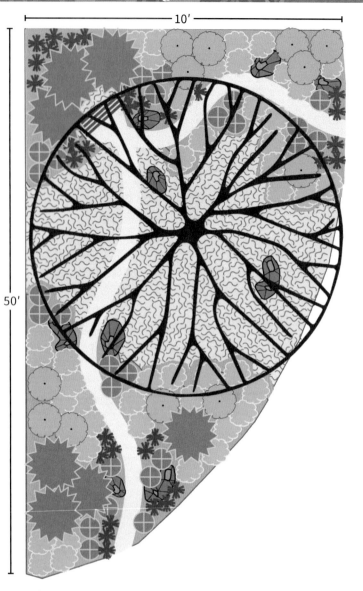

10'

50'

Lonomea (Sapindus oahuensis) is a beautiful shade tree, with leaves up to a foot long. It's easy to grow and maintain given full sun and well-drained soil. It's endemic to Kaua'i (where it's referred to as lonomea) and O'ahu (where it's also known as kaulu or aulu). For other islands, consider wiliwili (*Erythrina sandwicensis*, see the Coastal Arid design), or 'ohe makai (*Polyscias sandwicensis*, and for small yards pōkalakala (*Polyscias racemosa*, see Coastal Dry design). **Spacing:** allow a 35-40' canopy.

Ma'o hau hele (Hibiscus brackenridgei) is a beautiful hibiscus and the state flower of Hawai'i. The common name means "green traveling hau", referring to how this sprawling plant may topple over, root at the nodes, and form a new plant. Periodic pruning will prevent this. There are three subspecies and the quick reference guide shows their presence by island. This plant is sometimes prone to rose beetles which leave holes in the leaves. Leaving lights on from dusk to 8 or 9 pm can reduce their presence. **Spacing:** 3-6'

'A'ali'i (Dodonaea viscosa) is an attractive and reliable shrub (or small tree) that produces decorative papery seed capsules from red to cream in color. Note: plants sourced from seed from higher elevations will be larger and more tree-like, so inquire about origin. It can be used as an attractive specimen, an informal hedge or screen, and to stabilize soils on slopes or banks. It needs full sun, well-drained soil, and is very drought tolerant once established. Seed capsules are used in making lei and the wood was used to make small hand tools. **Spacing:** 4-7' (wider for higher elevation sources).

Kōʻokoʻolau *(Bidens species)* add bright color to the landscape with their showy yellow flowers. Their leaves can be used to make tea. Look for kōʻokoʻolau in the herb and shrub section in the quick reference guide to find species listed in the dry zone. Size is variable, even within species, but most respond well to pruning to make them more compact. The landscape photo features *Bidens menziesii* and the closeup features Bidens torta. **Spacing:** 1.5-3' depending on species

ʻIlieʻe *(Plumbago zeylanica)* is a great ground cover, especially useful for stabilizing soil to reduce erosion (and it's also unpalatable to goats). Use in place of wedelia and non-native plumbagos. Plants withstand heavy pruning and this helps keep them contained and encourages dense branching. It can be grown as a low hedge, or a more naturalized rambling shrub for larger areas as shown here. While it prefers full sun, it will tolerate partial shade better than many other plants suitable to dry conditions. **Spacing:** 2'-3'

Pōhinahina *(Vitex rotundifolia)* is an amazing, low-growing shrub and a workhorse, especially in tough urban environments where it can be seen thriving in narrow commercial strips or sidewalk medians. Plants produce showy light purple flowers. Leaves also emit a nice fragrance, almost sage-like. This is a dependable plant that is especially suited for the novice gardener. It responds well to pruning and will need periodic pruning as it will extend into the walkway. **Spacing:** 2-3'

Pili *(Heteropogon contortus)* is a tough, drought-tolerant grass and makes a great accent plant. While drought-tolerant, it will have a greener, more vibrant look with some additional moisture. Along with serving as an accent, it can be a groundcover when planted more densely. There are more upright and prostrate forms available. **Spacing:** 1.5-2'

If you know someone who claims that native plants are too difficult or unreliable, recommend ʻaʻaliʻi and pōhinahina to quickly change their mind. As noted, ʻaʻaliʻi is tough, relatively fast growing and the decorative seed capsules can provide nice color. It would be a great alternative to oleander or mockorange. Pōhinahina has lovely foliage, beautiful flowers and will fill an area quickly. It's a great alternative to the non-native (and invasive) lantana.

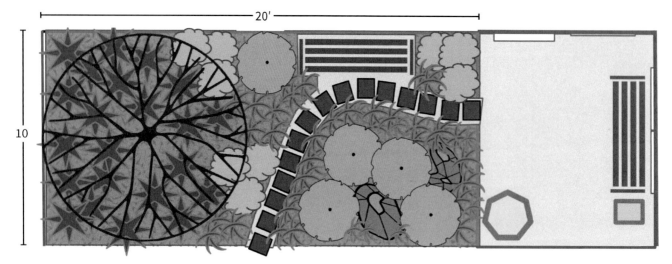

20'

10

'Ōhi'a lehua *(Metrosideros polymorpha)* is aptly named *polymorpha* as there are many forms, recognized as varieties, which play critical roles in almost all Hawaiian forests from low to high and wet to dry. Ecologically, these plants capture rain and provide habitat and food for birds like honeycreepers. Stunning flowers may be red, yellow, and orange. Blossoms and leaf tips are prized for lei. See the Resource Guide for more information on this incredible plant. **Spacing:** at least 5' (preferably more) from a fence line or building (this example space is a little small, but these plants are slow growing and can be pruned). **Alternatives:** Pāpala kēpau *(Ceodes brunoniana,* lovely but produces sticky fruit); Kauila *(Colubrina oppositifolia).*

'Ūlei *(Osteomeles anthyllidifolia)* is a tough and versatile shrub with attractive white flowers that have a lovely fragrance. It's adapted to a range of habitats and is drought tolerant, but will do best in full sun and needs well-drained soil. It can be left to stretch out and ramble, but it also responds well to pruning. **Spacing:** 3'

Palapalai *(Microlepia strigosa* var. *strigosa)* is a great fern for the understory, offering beautiful texture and form, as well as serving to suppress weeds. It's usually found in mesic forests, but can also occur in dry and wet forests. Culturally, this plant is valued for making lei. It's sacred to Laka, the goddess of hula and is used to adorn the hula altar. Palapalai appears in many songs and chants, reflecting its beauty and cultural significance. Note: this plant does best in partial shade. For properties on the drier end of a mesic zone (or during drought), it will benefit from some additional water until a canopy of shade develops. **Spacing:** 2' **Alternatives:** Kupukupu *(Nephrolepis cordifolia)* is an easy to grow fern, but it can be aggressive and will spread (be prepared to weed or plant where it has a natural barrier like a rock wall).

Kōʻokoʻolau (*Bidens* species) add bright color to the landscape with their showy yellow flowers and the leaves can be used to make tea. Look for kōʻokoʻolau (in both the herb and shrub section) in the quick reference guide to find a species listed in the mesic zone. Size is variable, even within species, but most respond well to pruning to make them more compact. The landscape photo features *Bidens micrantha* subsp. *micrantha* and the closeup features *Bidens torta*. **Spacing:** 1.5-3' depending on species.

ʻUkiʻuki (*Dianella sandwicensis*) is a great accent plant with delicately beautiful flowers. There's a short compact form (1-1.5' tall) with brilliant bluish-purple fruits; a taller, thinner-leafed one (3') with brownish-purple fruits; and a white-fruited form with paler green leaves. It naturally occurs in somewhat open to shaded sites usually in mesic forests, but also in dry shrubland, grassland on lava and in wet forests. **Spacing:** 1-2'

Hurricanes 'Iwa and 'Iniki destroyed half of the 60-70 remaining ālula plants along the Nā Pali Coast on Kauaʻi and 10 of the 12 plants in the Hāʻupu area. While preserving natural habitat should be the primary focus, putting endangered plants that are allowed in the horticultural trade in your landscape can help serve as a buffer against extinction.

Hala pepe (*Dracaena aurea, D. auwahiensis, D. forbesii, D. hawaiiensis*) adds a nice vertical accent to a lanai and it's a great alternative to money tree and other non-native dracenas. They produce beautiful displays of greenish yellow tubular flowers and decorative red berries. Find hala pepe in the tree section of the quick reference guide and whenever possible, select a species that naturally occurs where you live. **Alternatives:** palapalai (*Microlepia strigosa* var. *strigosa*) or ʻukiʻuki (*Dianella sandwicensis*).

Ālula (*Brighamia insignis*) are fairly easy to grow in pots in a partly sunny location, but MUST have a well-aerated soil mix (i.e. for succulents and cactus, or mixes containing black cinder) for perfect drainage and they do need frequent watering. If growing in the ground, again ensure excellent drainage (consider adding black cinder) in a partly sunny location and protect from slugs and snails. Flowers produce a sweet smell similar to honeysuckle or citrus. This plant is federally endangered.

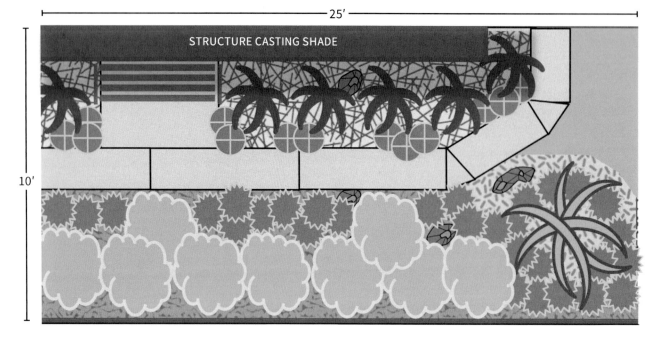

STRUCTURE CASTING SHADE

25'

10'

FOREST & KIM STARR

'Ākia (Wikstroemia uva-ursi) is a low-sprawling shrub with orange-red berries. It's drought tolerant, responds well to pruning and can easily be shaped into a denser, more compact form. It looks spectacular flowing over rocks or low walls. The flowers and decorative fruit are used for making lei haku. 'Ākia was used as a poison to stun fish, making them easy to catch. **Spacing:** 2-3'

Hala pepe (Dracaena aurea, D. auwahiensis, D. forbesii, D. hawaiiensis) may be slow growing, but it's worth the effort. It is a great alternative to the money tree and other non-native dracenas. Hala pepe produce beautiful displays of greenish yellow tubular flowers and decorative red berries. **Spacing:** allow a 6' width **Alternatives:** 'A'ali'i (Dodonaea viscosa).

FOREST & KIM STARR

Ki (Cordyline fruticosa) is a polynesian introduction with leaves used for thatch, food wrappers, hula skirts, and sandals. Plants do well in full sun or partial shade, and benefit from protection from the wind. Many varieties are available with various leaf colors, but the original Polynesian introduction was green. **Spacing:** 3-4'

FOREST & KIM STARR

Palapalai *(Microlepia strigosa var. strigosa)* is a great fern for a partially shady area, offering beautiful texture and form, as well as serving to suppress weeds. It's usually in mesic forests, but can also occur in dry and wet forests. Culturally, this plant is valued for making lei. It's sacred to Laka, the goddess of hula and is used to adorn the Hula altar. Palapalai appears in many songs and chants, reflecting its beauty and cultural importance. **Spacing:** 2'. **Alternatives:** Kupukupu *(Nephrolepis cordifolia)* is an easy to grow fern, but it can be aggressive and will spread (be prepared to weed or plant where it has a natural barrier like a rock wall).

'Ilima papa *(Sida fallax)* is a lovely plant with flower color spanning the yellow to orange spectrum and some forms with a dark red base. Note there are two forms: 'ilima and 'ilima papa and the lower growing 'ilima papa is recommended here. 'Ilima is typically from higher elevations, taller in stature and less drought tolerant. 'Ilima papa is a shorter, more drought-tolerant form from the lowlands. Heavy watering (like from an automated sprinkler system) will cause fungal rot or black sooty mold and plants will decline rapidly. This plant is the island flower of O'ahu and prized for making lei 'ilima. **Spacing:** 20-24"

Ihi'ihi *(Marsilea villosa)* is a unique fern with leaves like 4-leaf clovers. While it's endangered, it's relatively easy to grow, and spreads rapidly with periodic moisture. It's not essential to this design, but the showy leaves are a nice feature, and it will fill in empty spaces (reducing the need to weed). Although it's adapted to ephemeral wetlands or areas that are seasonally wet and then dry, it does not require this for survival (at UH Mānoa it's thriving at a native plant garden that gets some supplemental irrigation, but is never wet like an ephemeral pool). Watering may restore growth if it dries out. **Spacing:** 1' and plants will spread.

'Ala'ala wai nui *(Peperomia blanda var. floribunda, P. mauiensis, P. sandwicensis, P. tetraphylla)* are great as accents or in pots in partially shady locations. *Peperomia blanda* and *P. tetraphylla* are more drought tolerant and resistant to thrips. *Peperomia sandwicensis* has lovely foliage, but is very slow growing. All are generally pretty pest resistant, but watch for slugs. A gray green dye called 'ahiahia, or puahia for dying kapa was made from the ashes of this plant and it had numerous medicinal uses. **Spacing:** 1'

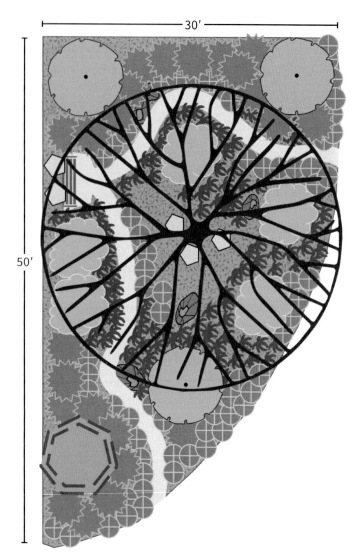

Manele (Sapindus saponaria) make beautiful shade trees. They naturally occur in mesic forests, typically at higher elevations, but they do well in low and dry urban areas as well. **Spacing:** allow a 40' width. **Alternatives:** Kauila (*Alphitonia ponderosa*) or Koa (*Acacia koa*) for upper elevation Maui and Hawai'i Island.

Hō'awa (Pittosporum species) are beautiful plants with lovely foliage and creamy white flowers that are especially fragrant at night. *Pittosporum confertiflorum* can grow as a shrub or a tree, the others shown in the quick reference table are more tree-like. **Spacing:** allow a 10' width.

'Alala, the Hawaiian crow (*Corvus tropicus*) fed on Ho'awa (*Pittosporum hosmeri*), helping to spread its seed. Sadly, 'alala is now extinct in the wild, negatively impacting this plant as well. This is an excellent example of the interdependence between plants and animals.

Koki'o ke'oke'o (Hibiscus arnottianus) is an attractive shrub with fragrant white flowers. Subspecies *arnottianus*, featured in the picture, has a red staminal column. Federally endangered subspecies *immaculatus* has a white staminal column and is a bit smaller, and subspecies *punaluuensis*, also with a white staminal column, is a bit larger. Plants may grow quite tall, upwards of 30', but can be pruned to make them bushier and more compact. **Spacing:** allow a 10' width. **Alternatives:** Ākia (*Wikstroemia oahuensis*) or koki'o kea (*Hibiscus waimeae*).

Māmaki (*Pipturus albidus*) is a lovely shrub (or occasionally small tree) with light to dark green leaves with pink to reddish veins (leaf color varies). Plants do best in the understory or in filtered, partially sunny locations (and suffer in hot, dry coastal settings). A medicinal tea can be made from the leaves. Māmaki is a host plant for the native Kamehameha Butterfly, similar to the non-native monarch, but with bolder designs. Avoid spraying this plant with any insecticides to protect the caterpillars (and yourself if you drink the tea). **Spacing:** allow a 10' width.

Palapalai (*Microlepia strigosa* var. *strigosa*) is a great fern for the understory, offering a beautiful texture and serving to suppress weeds. Culturally, this plant is valued for making lei. It's sacred to Laka, the goddess of hula, and is used to adorn the Hula altar. Note: this plant does best in partial shade. For properties on the drier end of a mesic zone (or during drought), it will benefit from some additional water until a canopy of shade develops. **Spacing:** 2-3'

'Ūlei (*Osteomeles anthyllidifolia*) is a hardy and versatile shrub with fragrant white flowers. It's naturally sprawling but can be pruned to make it more compact. It does best in full sun and needs well-drained soil. **Spacing:** 3'

Maile (*Alyxia stellata*) is a woody vine found in dry to mesic forests. It does best in partial shade and is recommended here at the base of the tree and on a trellis behind the bench. It's highly fragrant new growth is used to make beautiful lei.

'Uki'uki (*Dianella sandwicensis*) is a great accent plant with delicately beautiful flowers. There's a short compact form (1-1.5' tall) with brilliant bluish-purple fruits; a taller, thinner leafed one (3') with brownish-purple fruits; and a white-fruited form with paler green leaves. It naturally occurs in somewhat open to shaded sites usually in mesic forests (but also in dry shrubland, grassland on lava and in wet forests). **Spacing:** 1-2'

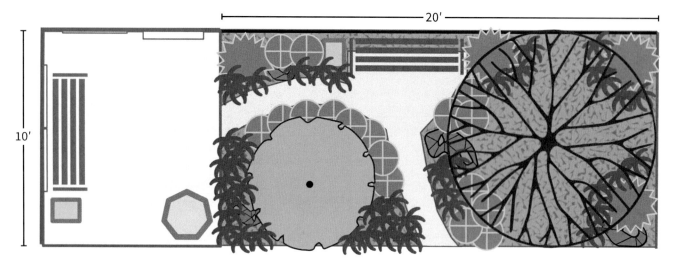

20'

10'

Ohe *(Polyscias hawaiensis [formerly Tetraplasandra])* is a beautiful and easy to grow tree. It occurs in mesic to wet forests. It may be narrow and tall or short and broad depending on origin. As it grows, it can develop a beautiful branching structure. Medicinally, lactating mothers would eat the fruit and it would cure the baby of pāʻaoʻao (physical weaknesses) and ʻea (thrush) with no side effects. **Spacing:** allow a 10' width. **Alternatives:** Hōʻawa *(Pittosporum confertiflorum, glabrum* or *hosmeri)*.

Kokiʻo keʻokeʻo *(Hibiscus arnottianus)* is a native hibiscus with stunning white flowers with a nice fragrance and three recognized subspecies. Subspecies arnottianus, featured in the picture, has a red staminal column. Federally endangered subspecies immaculatus has a white staminal column and is a bit smaller, and subspecies punaluuensis, also with a white staminal column, is a bit larger. Left unchecked, plants may grow quite tall, upwards of 30'. They benefit from some pruning to keep them bushier and more compact. **Alternatives:** Ākia *(Wikstroemia oahuensis)* which has jasmine scented flowers or Kokiʻo kea *(Hibiscus waimeae)*. **Spacing:** ideally allow an 8-10' width, but it can be pruned back to fit in smaller spaces.

ʻAwapuhi *(Zingiber zerumbet)* is a canoe plant with stunning flowers and grows well in partial to even full shade. While slow growing, like most gingers it will creep out and can take over if not managed. It dies back annually so best not to feature it as the specimen in a design. Traditionally, and at present, this plant is used in shampoos, both directly and processed (check your shampoo bottle!). **Spacing:** 2-3'

Neke *(Cyclosorus interruptus)* is a very attractive fern, about 2' tall, with beautiful fronds prized for making lei. An experienced native plant specialist and grower believes this plant is underrepresented and under-valued in the landscape industry and should be used more widely given its beauty. It will do well in this design for a wet zone as it naturally occurs along the margins of streams and in marshy areas. Spacing: 1-2'

'Uki'uki *(Dianella sandwicensis)* is a great accent plant with delicately beautiful flowers. There's a short compact form (1-1.5' tall) with brilliant bluish-purple fruits; a taller, thinner leafed one (3') with brownish-purple fruits; and a white-fruited form with paler green leaves. It naturally occurs in somewhat open to shaded sites usually in mesic forests (but also in dry shrubland, grassland on lava and in wet forests). In this design, it's recommended in the understory of the loulu. It would also look great in pots. As an accent, it could be placed periodically or continuously along the pathway, but the pōhinahina would need to be more vigilantly trimmed to not overtake it. **Spacing:** 1-2'

'Oha *(Delissea rhytidosperma)* is federally listed as endangered, but fortunately it's considered one of the easiest and most rewarding plants in the Lobelia family to grow. It does great in the shade of trees and will do well with neighboring ferns and other shrubs. The flowers are exquisitely shaped, a true work of art. While It naturally occurs at higher elevations, it does fine lower down, even in pots, given adequate drainage and filtered light. In a large pot, it would look beautiful planted with palapalai *(Microlepia strigosa* var *strigosa)* **Spacing:** allow 3-4 width.

Olena *(Curcuma longa)* is a canoe plant that has gorgeous flowers and medicinal benefits (roots are the source of turmeric, an anti-inflammatory). Plant rhizomes 4" deep. Note that plants will die back and go dormant during the winter. You could pair it with 'Ala'ala wai nui *(Peperomia sp.)* to provide cover while it's dormant (but not recommended if you plan to harvest the olena). **Spacing:** 2' **Alternatives:** 'Uki'uki *(Dianella sandwicensis)*, Neke *(Cyclosorus interruptus)*, 'Ala'ala wai nui *(Peperomia sp.)* all look great in containers.

inland wet   87

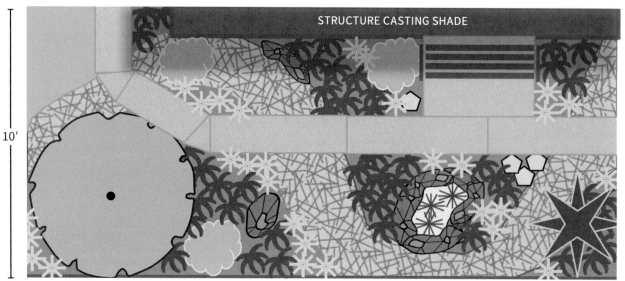

25'

10'

STRUCTURE CASTING SHADE

Hōʻawa (Pittosporum confertiflorum, P. glabrum, or P. hosmeri) are beautiful plants with lovely foliage and creamy white flowers that are especially fragrant at night. Pittosporum confertiflorum can grow as a shrub or a tree, the other species are more tree-like. **Spacing:** allow an 8-10' width. **Alternatives:** Kokiʻo kea (Hibiscus waimeae) or Loulu (Pritchardia beccariana, P. glabrata or P. martii all suitable for inland wet).

ʻOlena (Curcuma longa) is a canoe plant that has gorgeous flowers and medicinal benefits (roots are the source of turmeric, an anti-inflammatory). Plant rhizomes 4" deep. Note that plants will die back and go dormant during the dry season. Spacing: 1'

Neke (Cyclosorus interruptus) is a very attractive fern with lovely fronds prized for making lei. It should be used more widely given its beauty. Spacing: 1.5' Alternatives: Palapalai (Microlepia strigosa var. strigosa).

ʻAmaʻu (Sadleria cyatheoides or S. pallida) are beautiful ferns displaying bright red, magenta, to orange colors when fiddleheads (croziers) emerge to green upon maturity. Sadleria cyatheoides is a bit smaller and more drought tolerant. At high altitudes it does fine in full sun, but needs more protection in urban areas. ʻAmaʻu tends to tolerate drier, sunnier places than hāpuʻu. Spacing: allow 4-6' width. **Alternatives:** hapuʻu (Cibotium sp.) for larger spaces.

'Uki'uki *(Dianella sandwicensis)* is a great accent plant with delicately beautiful flowers. There's a short compact form (1-1.5' tall) with brilliant bluish-purple fruits; a taller, thinner leafed one (3') with brownish-purple fruits; and a white-fruited form with paler green leaves. It naturally occurs in somewhat open to shaded sites usually in mesic, but also wet forests. **Spacing:** 1-2'

Meyen's sedge *(Carex meyenii)* is a nice accent under tall shrubs or trees and does well in full sun. It's attractive as a groundcover when planted en masse and its blades are a bit less sharp than those of the O'ahu sedge (*C. wahuensis*). **Spacing:** 1.5'

This naturalized design depends on massing and subtle differences in foliage texture and color. If this is not your style, some bolder alternatives using canoe plants include swapping out the ho'awa for mai'a (banana); the kohekohe for kalo; and the 'oha for 'awapuhi. Please peruse the quick reference table, designed to be a useful tool to help you select the right plant for your property and tastes.

'Oha *(Delissea rhytidosperma)* is federally listed as endangered, but fortunately it's considered one of the easiest and most rewarding plants in the Lobelia family to grow. It does great in the shade of trees and will do well with neighboring ferns and other shrubs. The flowers are exquisitely shaped, a true work of art. While it occurs naturally at higher elevations, it does fine lower down, even in pots, given adequate drainage and filtered light. **Spacing:** 4'

Kohekohe *(Eleocharis obtusa)* would look lovely in the small water feature shown in this design. Plants do well in full to partial sun. **Spacing:** 1-2' **Alternatives:** see the sedges section in the quick reference table for many great alternatives such as Kaluhā (*Schoenoplectiella juncoides*), or Hawai'i sedge (*Carex alligata*).

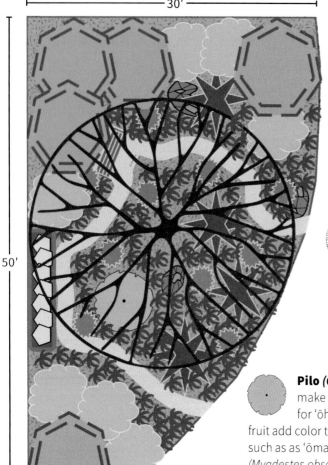

30'

50'

J.B. FRIDAY

DAVID EICKHOFF

ʻŌhiʻa lehua *(Metrosideros polymorpha)* is aptly named *M. polymorpha* as there are many forms, recognized as varieties, which play critical roles in almost all Hawaiian forests from ʌ to high and wet to dry. Ecologically, these plants capture rain and provide habitat and food for birds like honeycreepers. Stunning flowers may be red, yellow, or orange. Blossoms and leaf tips are prized for lei. See the Resource Guide for more information on this incredible plant. **Spacing:** allow a 25' canopy.

Pilo *(Coprosma rhynchocarpa)* make excellent understory trees for ʻōhiʻa and koa. Bright colored fruit add color to the landscape and birds such as as ʻōmaʻo or Hawaiian thrush *(Myadestes obscurus)* prize and guard trees bearing fruit. Plant when about one foot high (after about 6 months) and plants will flower and begin to fruit within five years. **Spacing:** allow a 10' width.

J.B. FRIDAY

Naupaka kuahiwi *(Scaevola chamissoniana)* is a mountain naupaka, naturally occuring at mid to high elevations. This species is faster growing than many other naupakas and is more fragrant than beach naupaka. White flowers bloom sporadically throughout the year and form a purple fleshy fruit with a central seed, a food for native birds. **Spacing:** 4-6'

DAVID EICKHOFF

DAVID EICKHOFF

Kokiʻo keʻokeʻo *(Hibiscus arnottianus)* is a beautiful hibiscus with stunning and fragrant white flowers. There are three recognized subspecies. Subspecies *arnottianus* has a red staminal column, the other two, subsp. *immaculatus* and subsp. *punaluuensis*, have white staminal columns. Left unchecked, plants may grow quite tall, upwards of 30' and they benefit from some pruning to keep them bushier and more compact. **Spacing:** 8'

FOREST & KIM STARR

FOREST & KIM STARR

Kalo *(Colocasia esculenta)*, a canoe plant, is one of the most important plants in Hawaiian culture. All parts of the plant except the stem are eaten. There are wetland and dryland varieties available (it's believed that early Hawaiians developed more than 150 cultivars of kalo). See the Resource Guide for information on growing it. In addition to kalo, that strip could be subdivided to include 'olena *(Curcuma longa)*, and/or ipu *(Lageneria siceraria,* or *L. vulgaris)*.

Hapu'u *(Cibotium glaucum, C. chamissoi* **or** *C. menziesii)* are stunning ferns that form an important component of the understory in moist mesic and wet forests, serving as habitat for germinating tree seedlings and hosting smaller ferns and epiphytes. They need slightly acidic, well-drained soil and plenty of moisture. Water the fronds as well as the center of the fern where new shoots emerge. All grow 1-2" per year in height, but fronds grow laterally more quickly. Hawaiian honeycreepers use the pulu (wool) to line their nests. Feral pigs are an ongoing threat. **Spacing:** Allow a 6-10' width. **Alternatives:** 'Ama'u *(Sadleria cyatheoides* or *S. pallida)*

Palapalai *(Microlepia strigosa* **var.** *strigosa)* is a great fern for the understory, offering a beautiful texture and serving to suppress weeds. Culturally, this plant is valued for making lei. **Spacing:** 2-3' **Alternatives** (or rather in addition to palapalai to add more low-growing plants for the understory and trailside): 'uki'uki *(Dianella sandwicensis)*; sedges like Meyen's sedge *(Carex meyenii)* or Hawaii Sedge *(Carex alligata)*; and neke *(Cyclosorus interruptus)*.

'Oha *(Delissea rhytidosperma)* is federally listed as endangered, but fortunately it's considered one of the easiest and most rewarding plants in the Lobelia family to grow. It does great in the shade of trees and will do well with neighboring ferns and other shrubs. The flowers are exquisitely shaped, a true work of art. While it occurs naturally at higher elevations, it does fine lower down, given adequate drainage and filtered light. **Spacing:** 4'

APPENDICES

FAQs

1. How do I use this book?
2. Where can I find native plants?
3. How can I get in touch with other like-minded 'plant people'?
4. Is it better to plant native plants together in a garden, as a "community"?
5. Do native plants need less water?
6. What does "drought-tolerant once established" mean?
7. Why are some plants listed in arid or dry zones, but they have high moisture needs in the QR table?
8. Do native plants need less fertilizer?
9. What is Rapid ʻŌhiʻa Death (ROD)?
10. How do I learn more about growing kalo?
11. Can native plants spread little fire ants?
12. Are native plants invasive?
13. How can I improve my gardening skills?
14. How do I determine what's eating my plant or making it sick?

1. How do I use this book? This publication is intended to help you put "the right plant in the right place", or more specifically, select native Hawaiian or canoe plants that are adapted to the environmental conditions where you live and that have the landscape attributes you need. If you're in a hot, dry, low-elevation spot with little moisture, selecting a plant adapted to wet, high-elevation forests will make that plant pretty unhappy (and then you as well). Yet the small state of Hawaiʻi has more climate zones than most countries in the world. To assist you, we've provided maps featuring eight climate zones for each populated island. Determine the zone you're in and then refer to the quick reference table organized by plant type and showing plant presence or absence in these eight climate zones. The table also includes key information for plant selection such as each plant's ideal sun exposure, moisture needs, height, and width and potential function in the landscape (groundcover, screen/hedge, specimen etc.). Lastly, for each climate zone we provided designs including 6-8 plants in three common landscaping scenarios:

1. A small area off a lanai (including potted plants for the lanai);
2. A walkway (appropriate for a residential or commercial space), with half of the plants in partial shade; and
3. A yard large enough for a tree and accompanying shrubs and groundcovers.

None of these scenarios will look exactly like your property, but we hope they will help you generate ideas, and you can adapt some or all of the suggested combinations to your property.

2. Where can I find native plants? See our list of native plant nurseries by island after the next section, "Native Plant Ethics". And please read "Native Plant Ethics" to learn about the permits required and protocol to follow to collect native seeds in the wild. We generally don't encourage this in order to support hard working nurseries as well as to avoid endangering populations by over collecting.

3. How can I get in touch with other, "like-minded" gardeners, designers, "plant people?" Our Community Portal: www.gonativeplants.org. The community portal will enable you to communicate regularly with others interested in landscaping with native and canoe plants. You will be able to ask questions, get to know others, post pictures of successes and challenges and share what you're up to. We plan to organize speakers, coordinate plant exchanges, and share interesting articles.

4. Is it better to plant native plants together in a garden, as a "community," rather than as individual plants? While most people don't think of plants as being social creatures like humans, they do form relationships. For example, sandalwood benefits from a host plant (uses modified roots to draw nutrients from other plants' roots). Plants in the Fabaceae (aka legume) family fix nitrogen in the soil, making it available to other plants. A sapling with some companion plants around it to buffer the wind, provide some leaf litter to cool the soil and reduce moisture loss will generally do better than a sapling planted in bare soil with no surrounding plants. Yet, plants can also form competitive relationships, excluding neighbors from sunlight, reducing available moisture or nutrients. In the design section, we have tried to select a diversity of plants that will fill available niches, but not dominate the site. By starting with a diverse assemblage, if one plant struggles or naturally waxes and wanes (like pua kala), there will be other desirable species to fill in. Meanwhile, you as the gardener can direct the trajectory, pruning back the pōhinahina or routinely thinning the kupukupu, for example.

5. Do native plants need less water? Native plants have a range of water needs. This publication is designed to help you find plants that are adapted to the average temperature and precipitation levels where you live. Plant what is appropriate for where you live and once established, the plants should need supplemental irrigation only during drought. However, please keep in mind that local environmental conditions will have a huge impact as well. A shrub in a sidewalk median strip with concrete on either side will need more water than a shrub in a deep rich soil shaded by other plants.

6. A plant is listed in the arid zone in the quick reference table, but notes in the design section say it is very drought-tolerant 'once established.' What does this mean? No matter how drought tolerant they may be, almost all plants need regular watering initially to get established. This may be for 1-6 months depending on a number of factors such as the species, soil conditions, and seasonal climate at the time of planting. Start to taper back gradually, and monitor how the plant responds.

7. Why are some plants listed in arid or dry zones, but they have high moisture needs in the QR table? Some coastal plants are in arid or dry zones, but their water values are not correspondingly low. These are plants, mostly sedges and rushes, that are adapted to freshwater pools in otherwise arid or dry areas. They like their wet feet, but need full sun. For example, makaloa *(Cyperus laevigatus)*, is listed in coastal arid and dry zones, but has a moisture value of 4-5. If you're planting it in an arid or dry zone, do so where fresh water naturally accumulates. Another reason some plants may be zoned in arid or dry conditions, but have high moisture needs, is because they are able to access a fresh water lens. Groundwater near the coast accumulates and does not mix with salt water beneath it. Some plants like niu *(Cocos nucifera)* or hala *(Pandanus tectorius)* utilize this, meaning they still need moderate amounts of water but can survive in areas with low precipitation. If you're to plant coconut or hala in a coastal setting in an arid or dry zone, plant near sea level to enable these plants to access the fresh water lens.

8. Do native plants need less fertilizer (thereby saving me money and reducing negative impacts on the watershed)? Anecdotally, native plants may do better with less or no fertilizer. Many gardeners have observed that native plants given fertilizer thrive for a short period after developing lush leaves and then are quickly decimated by pests in contrast to unfertilized plants. Most horticultural plants that you purchase at a nursery have been selectively bred to thrive in conditions in residential landscapes which typically include additions of fertilizer. Yet native plants have adapted over millions of years with no such treatment. However, they also were in soils far different from a residential landscape – soils rich with microbial life and often including microorganisms critical for their survival. So what's the best way forward? We encourage you to cut back on fertilizers if this is a routine procedure for you and to leave more organic matter in your yard to let soils develop organically. However, everyone has a different aesthetic. If yours is a highly manicured one, it doesn't mean you can't use native plants. Do some experimenting and record what works (and please share your results on the Community Portal).

9. What is Rapid ʻŌhiʻa Death (ROD)? Rapid ʻŌhiʻa Death is a fungal disease that is relatively new to the islands and is killing ʻōhiʻa lehua trees. ʻŌhiʻa is the most abundant native tree in the islands and provides numerous ecosystem services (habitat and food for birds, serving as a nurse plant for other plants, "catching rain"), making the impacts of this disease dire. How does it spread? Humans are thought to be the major vector when they move infected wood or contaminated tools, gear and vehicles from one location to another. Feral ungulates and beetles are also potential vectors. To protect trees you plant and to prevent inadvertently spreading it while hiking or recreating, please follow these practices:

- Keep planting ʻōhiʻa! If properly cared for, planted ʻōhiʻa trees are unlikely to be affected by ROD.

- The more aggressive species of the two fungi that cause Rapid ʻŌhiʻa Death is widespread on Hawaiʻi Island and occurs on Kauaʻi but has not been detected on Oʻahu, Maui, Molokaʻi, or Lanaʻi *(Ceratocystis huliohia* and *C. lukuohia* are the two species with the latter being more aggressive).

- The fungi that cause ROD enter the tree through wounds. Protect your trees from injuries from string trimmers or lawnmowers. Many of the cases of ROD in urban settings on Hawaii Island were due to obvious injuries from weed trimmers or in some cases feral cats using the trees as scratching posts. The best practice is to control weeds around the tree with a layer of wood chips or other mulch.

- Don't run over roots with a lawn mower. The fungi can get in roots if they are scalped by machinery.

- The fungi do not seem to move through the soil into healthy roots, so even if the disease is nearby it does not seem to affect planted seedlings unless they are damaged.

- If you must prune a branch, use a pruning sealer on the cut. Use good pruning techniques.

- Don't move ʻōhiʻa wood or ʻōhiʻa parts.

- Don't transport ʻōhiʻa inter-island.

- Clean gear and tools, including shoes and clothes, before and after entering forests.

- Wash the tires and undercarriage of your vehicle to remove all soil or mud.

- Go to https://cms.ctahr.hawaii.edu/rod/ to find out more.

10. How do I learn more about growing kalo?

- "How to Harvest and Replant Kalo (Taro)" is a comprehensive review of all aspects of this plant, from the cultural to growing and preparing. To access, go to https://tinyurl.com/wyj536s and then click 'Huki kalo, kalo kanu'. While written for children (a 4th grade classroom), it's a great resource.

- *The Wondrous Kalo Plant* by Duke Morgan of northshorenews.com offers a oncise overview.

- For information about the numerous varieties available see Taro Varieties in Hawaii: https://www.ctahr.hawaii.edu/Site/Taro.aspx.

- *The Hawaiian planter* by E.S. Craighill Handy is a valuable and unique ethnobotanical overview of taro including details on growing dry and wet taro. The full citation is: Handy, E. S. Craighill (Edward Smith Craighill), 1892-1980. The Hawaiian Planter. Honolulu, Hawaii: The Museum, 1940.
- See https://www.kupunakalo.com/ "the online resource and reconnection with kalo, the food that sustained our ancestors."

11. Can native plants spread little fire ants? In some cases, nursery plants have been vectors for little fire ants. Be careful to buy only from reputable vendors. To learn more about fire ants, go to https://dlnr.hawaii.gov/hisc/info/invasive-species-profiles/little-fire-ant/.

12. Are native plants invasive? Native plants are not invasive, but some are more aggressive than others, like neneleau (*Rhus sandwicensis*). While it may be very aggressive locally (filling the area where it's planted and sending root suckers out into nearby areas), this is different from being invasive—spreading far beyond where it's planted and displacing native species (like invasive strawberry guava, for example). If you or someone you know is considering using a non-native species, a great place to check whether it's invasive or not is Plantpono.org.

13. How can I improve my gardening skills? Check out these sites:

- Master Gardener FAQ: https://www.ctahr.hawaii.edu/UHMG/FAQ/index.asp
- Master Gardener Gardening Basics: https://www.ctahr.hawaii.edu/UHMG/HI-garden-basics.asp
- Maui County's Landscape and Gardening Handbook: https://www.mauicounty.gov/DocumentCenter/View/15460/Handbook-Publication

14. How do I determine what's eating my plant or making it sick?

- Check out this Master Gardener link: https://www.ctahr.hawaii.edu/UHMG/FAQ/index.asp.
- Post a question (ideally with pictures), on our Community Portal: www.gonativeplants.org.

Other useful links

- **http://nativeplants.hawaii.edu/**
  incredible resource on landscape attributes of native Hawiian plants.
- **http://hawaiiannativeplants.com/ourplants**
  landscape uses and care of native Hawaiian and canoe plants.
- **http://www.nativehawaiiangarden.org/home**
  by Bruce Koebele, coauthor of *A Native Hawaiian Garden: How to Grow and Care For Island Plants*
- **https://plantpono.org/**
  use to determine whether non-native plants are invasive
  (also allows you to search and filter all landscaping plants by feature like color and growth form)
- **http://www.starrenvironmental.com/images**
  photos of native Hawaiian plants
- **https://laukahi.org/types-of-ohia/**
  information on 'Ōhi'a taxa, and identifying varieties
- **TraditionalTree.org and https://agroforestry.org/free-publications/traditional-tree-profiles**
  information on Traditional Trees of the Pacific Islands: Culture, Environment and Use
- **https://www.ctahr.hawaii.edu/oc/freepubs/pdf/L-2.pdf**
  helpful tips on watering trees
- **https://naturalhistory2.si.edu/botany/hawaiianflora**
  updated taxonomy of all plants, native or non-native, that grow in Hawai'i

PLANTING NATIVES FOR POLLINATORS
- **https://www.pollinator.org/PDFs/Guides/HawaiianIsland.EcoRegGuide.FINAL.hi-res.pdf**
  Selecting Plants for Pollinators, see page 16 for a list of native species and their pollinators
- **https://www.xerces.org/pollinator-resource-center/hawaii**
  Pollinator Conservation Resources: Hawai'i
- **https://xerces.org/sites/default/files/2018-05/15-029_03_XercesSoc_HabitatInstallGuide_Pacific-Islands-Area_web.pdf**
  Habitat Planting for Pollinators: Pacific Islands Area

FIREWISE LANDSCAPING
- **https://www.hawaiiwildfire.org/fire-resource-library-blog/rsg-your-personal-wildland-fire-action-guide**
  Hawaii Island Firewise Guide by HWMO (Hawaii Wildfire Management Organization)
- **https://www.pacificfireexchange.org/weed-fire-risk-assessments**
  Weed Risk Fire Database
- **NFPA.org and firewise.org (link too long to insert here but search online for the above)**
  Firewise Guide to Landscape and Construction

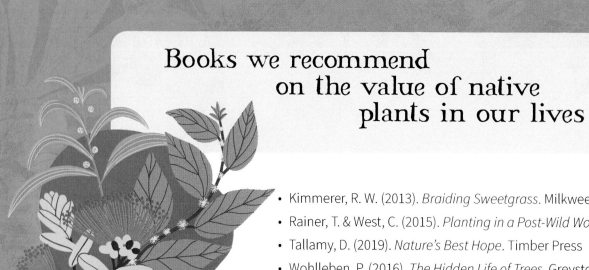

Books we recommend on the value of native plants in our lives

- Kimmerer, R. W. (2013). *Braiding Sweetgrass.* Milkweed Editions
- Rainer, T. & West, C. (2015). *Planting in a Post-Wild World.* Timber Press
- Tallamy, D. (2019). *Nature's Best Hope.* Timber Press
- Wohlleben, P. (2016). *The Hidden Life of Trees.* Greystone Books

Plant Nursery List

Island	Name	Address	Phone	Website or Email	Notes
Hawaiʻi	Aikane Nursery	P.O. Box 459, Kapaʻau, HI 96755	(808) 430-8198	aikanenursery.com	
Hawaiʻi	Aileen's Nursery	942 W. Kawailani Street Hilo, HI 96720	(808) 936-2671		M-F, 7:30 am to 5:30 pm, by appointmentt only.
Hawaiʻi	Elemental Plants	44-2600 Hawaii Belt Hwy, Honokaa, HI 96727	(808) 640-2506	https://kiva.org/lend/1812591	
Hawaiʻi	ESP	PO Box 905 Kamuela, HI 96743	(808) 885-7418	esp905@hawaiiantel.net	Kamauela Saturday Market or by appointment.
Hawaiʻi	Future Forests Nursery	Po Box 847 Kailua-Kona, HI 96745	(808) 325-2377	trees@forestnursery.com	Wide selection of native plants. By appt. only.
Hawaiʻi	Garden Exchange	300 Keawe St. Hilo, HI 96720	(808) 961-2875	gardenexchangehilo.com	
Hawaiʻi	Hawaiian Reforestation Program	Mountain View, HI 96771	(808) 769-0683	1sandalwoodman@gmail.com	By appointment.
Hawaiʻi	Home Depot Kona	73-5598 Olowalu St, Kailua-Kona, HI 96740	(808) 326-6013	homedepot.com	
Hawaiʻi	ʻIli Kupono Gardens	73-4261 Lauʻi St., Kona, Hi 96740	(808) 989-0323	cazdimarco@gmail.com	
Hawaiʻi	Kealakekua Forest Nursery Native Contract Nursery		(808) 785-8991	katrina_isch@forestsolutionsinc.com	By appointment.
Hawaiʻi	Lehua Lena Nursery	PO Box 1479, Keaʻau HI 96749	(808) 938-4179	lehualenanursery@gmail.com lehualenanursery.com	Minimum order.
Hawaiʻi	Mauna Ikena	P.O. Box 1337, Keaʻau HI 96749	(808) 966-6337	maunaikena@gmail.com	Minimum order.
Hawaiʻi	Niu Loa Hiki	PO Box 206 Naʻalehu, HI 96772	(808) 937-6305	kausideman@yahoo.com	By appointment.
Hawaiʻi	Pacific ʻAina Management, LLC, serving the West Side	68-4747 Queen Kaahumanu Highway, Kamuela, HI 96743	(808) 437-7500	plants@pacainamgmt.com	By appointment.
Hawaiʻi	Paradise Plants Home & Garden	40 Wiwoʻole St. Hilo, HI 96720	808) 935-4043	paradiseplantshilo.com	

Island	Name	Address	Phone	Website or Email	Notes
Hawaiʻi	State Tree Nursery, Division of Forestry and Wildlife, DLNR	Kamuela	(808) 974-4221	http://dlnr.hawaii.gov/forestry/info/nurseries/	Minimum order.
Hawaiʻi	Tropical Edibles	89-5696 Mamalahoa Hwy, Capt. Cook, HI 96704	(808) 328-0420	tropicaledibles@gmail.com	
Kauaʻi	Home Depot	4320 Nuhou St. Lihue, HI 96766	(808) 632-2740	homedepot.com	
Kauaʻi	Kauaʻi Nursery & Landscaping	3-1550 Kaumualiʻi Hwy., Lihue, HI 96766	(808) 245-7747	kauainursery.com	
Kauaʻi	Kauaʻi Seascapes Nursery	4741 Kahiliholo Rd. #A, Kilauea, HI 96754	(808) 828-0444	kauaiseascapesnursery.com	
Kauaʻi	Keep it Native	Kauaʻi	(808) 742-9894	kerinr@hawaiiantel.net	Minimum order, native plants only.
Maui	Hoʻolawa	3 Kahiapo Place, Haiku, HI 96708	(808) 283-9154	hoolawafarms.com	
Maui	Maui Native Nursery	1267 Naʻalae Rd. Kula, HI 96790	(808) 878-8276	https://www.mauinativenursery.com/sales-policy.html	Retail sales through WalMart, Lowe's, Home Depot and True Value. Sales at nursery, min. $50.
Maui	Maui Nui Botanical Gardens	150 Kanaloa Avel, Kahului, HI 96732	(808) 249-2798	www.mnbg.org	Plant sales on Thursdays, giveaways on Fridays, limited variety of plants. Kamaʻaina & children free admission.
Molokaʻi	Molokai Land Trust	1800 Farrington Avenue, Kualapuu, HI 96757	(808) 553-5626	molokailandtrust.org	Limited walk-in sales, and contract growing of Molokai native plant material.
Molokaʻi	Wiliwili Hawaiian Plants	PO Box 535, Hoʻolehua HI 96729	(808) 567-6761 Cell: (808) 542-4651	wiliwili.hawaiianplants@gmail.com	Native plants only, minimum order 1,000.
Oʻahu	City Mill			citymill.com	See web site for locations.
Oʻahu	Contemporary Landscaping	41-758 Waikupanaha St. Waimanalo, HI 96795	(808) 343-4624	contemporarylandscapingllc.com	
Oʻahu	Home Depot	421 Alakawa St. Honolulu, HI 96817	(808) 521-7355	homedepot.com	
Oʻahu	Home Depot	4600 Kapolei Pkwy. Kapolei HI 96707	(808) 674-6120	homedepot.com	
Oʻahu	Hui Ku Maoli Ola	46-403 Haiku Rd, Kaneohe, HI 96744	(808) 235-6165	hawaiiannativeplants.com	All native or Polynesian introductions
Oʻahu	Koʻolau Farmers	1199 Dillingham Blvd., C109, Honolulu, HI. 96017	(808) 843-0436	koolaufarmers.com	Many native and Polynesian introductions.
Oʻahu	Koʻolau Farmers	45-580 Kamehameha Hwy Kaneohe, HI 96744	(808) 247-3911	koolaufarmers.com	Many native and Polynesian introductions.
Oʻahu	Koʻolau Farmers	1127 Kailua Rd. Kailua, HI 96734	(808) 263-4414	koolaufarmers.com	Many native and Polynesian introductions.
Oʻahu	Lyon Arboretum	3860 Manoa Rd. Honolulu, HI 96822	(808) 988-0456	https://manoa.hawaii.edu/lyon/classes-and-events/annual-plant-sales/	Annual Spring plant sale, reservations required.
Oʻahu	Maoli Farms	Oʻahu	(808) 452-4837	https://maolifarms.weebly.com/	
Oʻahu	Native Ecosystem Services LLC	47-104 Hunaahi Street, Kaneohe, HI 96774		nativeecosystemservices@gmail.com nativeecosystemservices.com	Minimum order
Oʻahu	Waimea Valley	59-864 Kamehameha Hwy., Haleiwa, HI 96712	(808) 638-5875	waimeavalley.net	Plant sale Saturday 8-12 AM. No admission fee if only buying plants.

Native Plant Ethics

The information below is from a "BUY NATIVES, IT MATTERS" poster by the Landscape Industry Council of Hawai'i (LICH). For items 4-6, we encourage people to purchase native plants from reputable nurseries rather than collecting seed on their own. This supports nurseries as well as preventing overharvesting of plant material that may endanger plant populations.

1. Golden rule: Use of native plants should never endanger their wild populations.

2. Do not collect native plants from state forests without a Department of Land and Natural Resources permit (http://dlnr.hawaii.gov/dofaw/permits/). Collection from national parks and wildlife refuges is usually not permitted. Any collection from private lands should only be done with the permission of the landowner.

3. Cultivating and selling threatened and endangered (T&E) species requires a license from the Hawai'i Department of Land and Natural Resources – Division of Forestry and Wildlife. Any T&E plants for sale in nurseries should must have a red T&E plant tag.

4. Collect native plants only if you are a trained individual. Native ground cover vegetation can be damaged very easily. Avoid unnecessary damage to collection sites by staying on or near established trails.

5. When collecting common species with a permit, collect less than 5% of total seeds from each plant.

6. When collecting, propagating and planting native plants, replicate nature's genetic diversity. Ideally, collect from 5-10 plants per population and a total of 3-5 populations. Keep good records of the location and condition of parent plants. Note provenance of plants throughout propagation to installation.

7. Use native plants from your island even if the species distribution is statewide.

8. Avoid moving native plants interisland.

9. Do not import native plants from outside Hawai'i.

10. Purchase native plants from an established plant nursery.

11. Use native plants in your landscaping only and do not outplant in natural areas unless the project is a planned native ecosystem restoration and the plants are grown specifically for that purpose.

Bibliography

Abbott, I. A. (1992). *La'au Hawai'i: Traditional Hawaiian uses of plants.* Bishop Museum Press.

Athens, J.S., Reith, T. M. & Dye, T. S (2014). *A paleoenvironmental and archaeological model-based age estimate for the colonization of Hawai'i.* American Antiquity 79(1) 144-155.

Baldos, O. C., & Antesco, D. K. (2022). *Jacquemontia sandwicensis 'leeward community college white', a versatile groundcover and hanging basket plant.* HortScience, 57(1), 22–23. https://doi.org/10.21273/hortsci16170-21

Barboza, Rick (2022). *Hui ku maoli ola: Our plants* (accessed numerous times in 2021, 2022) http://hawaiiannativeplants.com/ourplants/

Bezona, Norman, et at (2021). *Salt and wind tolerance of landscape plants for Hawai'i.* Cooperative Extension Service, College of Tropical Agriculture & Human Resources, University of Hawai'i Manoa https://www.ctahr.hawaii.edu/oc/freepubs/pdf/L-13.pdf

Bornhorst, H. L., & Rauch, F. D. (2003). *Native Hawaiian plants for landscaping, conservation, and reforestation.* Hawai'i Cooperative Extension Service, College of Tropical Agriculture and Human Resources, University of Hawai'i at Mānoa.

Bornhorst, H. L. (2005). *Growing Hawaiian plants: A how-to guide for the gardener.* Bess Press.

Carlquist, S. (1980). *Hawaii a natural history: Geology, climate, native flora and fauna above shoreline.* SB Printers, Inc.

Culliney J. L. & Koebele, B. P. (1999). *A native Hawaiian garden: How to grow and care for island plants.* University of Hawai'i Press.

Gustafson, R.J., Hebst, D.R. & Rundel, P. W. (2014). *Hawaiian plant life vegetation and flora.* University of Hawaii Press.

Holdsworth, G. A. B., Lincoln, N. K., & Dyke, P. V. (2009). *Amy Greenwell garden ethnobotanical guide to native Hawaiian plants & Polynesian-introduced plants.* Bishop Museum Press.

Kapi'olani Community College (Kapi'olaniCC) and Leeward Community College (LeewardCC) (2009). Native Plants Hawaii. Retrieved 2021-April 2022, from http://nativeplants.hawaii.edu/.

Krauss, B. H. (1993) *Plants in Hawaiian culture.* University of Hawai'i Press.

Maui Cultural Lands, (2015). *Hoawa: Pittosporum hosmeri.* Retrieved June 2022, from https://mauiculturallands.org/hoawa

Price, J. P., Jacobi, J. D., Gon, S. M. III, Matsuwaki, D., Mehrhoff, L., Wagner, W., Lucas, M., & Rowe, B. (2012). *Mapping plant species ranges in the Hawaiian Islands: Developing a methodology and associated GIS layers.* Open-File Report. https://doi.org/10.3133/ofr20121192

Rainer, T., & West, C. (2015). *Planting in a post-wild world: Designing plant communities for resilient landscapes.* Timber Press.

Rosenberger, K.E. (2016). *Growing Hawai'i's native plants: A simple step-by-step approach*, revised edition. Mutual Publishing.

Sohmer, S.H. & Gustafson, R. (1987). *Plants and flowers of Hawai'i.* University of Hawai'i Press.

Wagner, W. L., D. R. Herbst, and S. H. Sohmer. 1999. *Manual of the flowering plants of Hawai'i, Volumes I and II, revised edition*. Honolulu: University of Hawai'i Press.

Ziegler, A.C. (2002) *Hawaiian natural history, ecology and evolution*. University of Hawai'i Press.

INDEX

In place of a regular index, Table 1 on the following page is to help you find what plants are included in the Quick Reference (QR) Table, whether you're searching for them by Hawaiian name/common name or scientific name. Plant form is included so you know where to find it in the QR Table (organized by ferns, grasses, sedges/rushes, shrubs, trees, vines, and then alphabetized by Hawaiian name). To determine if a plant is in a design (Chapter 4), refer to Table 2, page 107.

Note on plant form: some canoe plants are listed under a plant form that is not technically correct, but is where we assume people would look for the plant based on its stature. For example, mai'a (banana) is technically an herb, but is listed under trees. If you were hoping a plant would be in this book, but didn't see it in the Quick Reference Table, search for it here by common name or scientific name and you may find it's included, but not under the form you were expecting.

TABLE 1. Hawaiian and scientific names and the form they're listed under in the Quick Reference Table

Name	Corresponding Scientific or Common Name	Plant Form as listed in Quick Reference Table
'A'ali'i	*Dodonaea viscosa*	Shrub
Abutilon menziesii	Ko'oloa 'ula	Shrub
Acacia koa	Koa	Tree
Acacia koaia	Koai'a	Tree
Achyranthes splendens var. rotundata	'Ahinahina	Shrub
Achyranthes splendens var. splendens	'Ahinahina	Shrub
Ae 'ae	*Bacopa monnieri*	Herb
'Ahinahina	*Achyranthes splendens var. rotundata*	Shrub
'Ahinahina	*Achyranthes splendens var. splendens*	Shrub
'Āhinahina	*Artemisia australis*	Shrub
'Āhinahina	*Artemisia mauiensis*	Shrub
'Ahu'awa	*Cyperus javanicus*	Sedge/Rush
'Aka'akai	*Schoenoplectus tabernaemontani*	Sedge/Rush
'Ākala	*Rubus hawaiensis*	Shrub
'Ākia	*Wikstroemia monticola*	Shrub
'Ākia	*Wikstroemia oahuensis*	Shrub
'Ākia	*Wikstroemia uva-ursi*	Shrub
'Aki'aki	*Sporobolus virginicus*	Grass
'Akiohala	*Hibiscus furcellatus*	Shrub
'Akoko	*Euphorbia celastroides var. celastroides*	Shrub
'Akoko	*Euphorbia degeneri*	Shrub
'Ākulikuli	*Sesuvium portulacastrum*	Herb
'Ala'ala wai nui	*Peperomia blanda var. floribunda*	Herb
'Ala'ala wai nui	*Peperomia mauiensis*	Herb
'Ala'ala wai nui	*Peperomia sandwicensis*	Herb
'Ala'ala wai nui	*Peperomia tetraphylla*	Herb
'Ala'ala wai nui wahine	*Plectranthus parviflorus*	Herb
Alahe'e	*Psydrax odorata*	Tree
Alena, nena	*Boerhavia repens*	Herb
Aleurites moluccana	Kukui	Tree
Alphitonia ponderosa	Kauila	Tree
Ālula	*Brighamia insignis*	Shrub
Alyxia stellata	Maile	Vine
'Ama'u	*Sadleria cyatheoides*	Fern
'Ama'u	*Sadleria pallida*	Fern
'Ānapanapa	*Colubrina asiatica*	Shrub
'Ānaunau	*Lepidium bidentatum var. o-waihiense*	Herb
Antidesma pulvinatum	Hame	Tree
Argemone glauca	Pua kala	Herb
Artemisia australis	'Āhinahina	Shrub
Artemisia mauiensis	'Āhinahina	Shrub
Artocarpus altilis	'Ulu	Tree
Astelia menziesiana	Pa'iniu	Herb
Auhuhu	*Tephrosia purpurea*	Shrub
Āulu	*Rockia sandwicensis*	Tree
'Awapuhi	*Zingiber zerumbet*	Herb
'Āweoweo	*Chenopodium oahuense*	Shrub
'Āwikiwiki	*Canavalia galeata*	Vine
'Āwikiwiki	*Canavalia hawaiiensis*	Vine
'Āwikiwiki	*Canavalia pubescens*	Vine
Bacopa monnieri	Ae 'ae	Herb
Banana (Mai'a)	*Musa acuminata*	Tree (tree-like)
Bidens amplectans	Kō'oko'olau	Herb
Bidens cosmoides	Po'olā nui	Herb
Bidens hawaiensis	Kō'oko'olau	Herb
Bidens hillebrandiana	Kō'oko'olau	Herb
Bidens menziesii subsp. *filiformis*	Kō'oko'olau	Shrub
Bidens menziesii subsp. *menziesii*	Kō'oko'olau	Shrub
Bidens micrantha subsp. *micrantha*	Kō'oko'olau	Herb
Bidens torta	Kō'oko'olau	Herb
Bird's nest fern	*Asplenium nidus*	Fern
Boerhavia repens	Alena, nena	Herb
Bolboschoenus maritimus	Kaluhā	Sedge/Rush
Bonamia	*Bonamia menziesii*	Vine
Bonamia menziesii	Bonamia	Vine
Brighamia insignis	Ālula	Shrub
Calophyllum inophyllum	Kamani	Tree
Canavalia galeata	'Āwikiwiki	Vine
Canavalia hawaiiensis	'Āwikiwiki	Vine
Canavalia pubescens	'Āwikiwiki	Vine
Capparis sandwichiana	Maiapilo	Shrub
Carex alligata	Hawai'i sedge	Sedge/Rush
Carex meyenii	Meyen's sedge	Sedge/Rush
Carex wahuensis subsp. *wahuensis*	O'ahu sedge	Sedge/Rush
Cenchrus agrimonioides var. *agrimonioides*	Kāmanomano	Grass
Ceodes brunoniana (formerly *Pisonia*)	Pāpala kēpau	Tree
Ceodes umbellifera (formerly *Pisonia*)	Āulu	Tree
Charpentiera obovata	Pāpala	Tree

Name	Corresponding Scientific or Common Name	Plant Form as listed in Quick Reference Table
Charpentiera ovata var. niuensis	Pāpala	Tree
Chenopodium oahuense	ʻĀweoweo	Shrub
Cheriodendron t rigynum	ʻŌlapa	Tree
Cibotium chamissoi	Hāpuʻu	Fern
Cibotium glaucum	Hāpuʻu pulu	Fern
Cibotium menziesii	Hāpuʻu ʻiʻi	Fern
Cladium jamaicense	ʻUki	Sedge/Rush
Clermontia arborescens	ʻŌhā wai nui	Shrub
Clermontia clermontioides	Hāhā	Shrub
Clermontia kakeana	ʻŌhā	Shrub
Coccolus orbiculatus	Huehue	Vine
Cocos nucifera	Niu	Tree
Colocasia esculenta	Kalo	Herb
Colubrina asiatica	ʻĀnapanapa	Shrub
Colubrina oppositifolia	Kauila	Tree
Coprosma ernodeoides	Kūkaenēnē	Shrub
Coprosma rhynchocarpa	Pilo, Hupilo	Tree
Cordia subcordata	Kou	Tree
Cordyline fruticosa	Ki	Shrub
Curcuma longa	ʻOlena	Herb
Cyclosorus hudsonianus	Laukahi	Fern
Cyclosorus interruptus	Neke	Fern
Cyperus javanicus	ʻAhuʻawa	Sedge/Rush
Cyperus laevigatus	Makaloa	Sedge/Rush
Cyperus trachysanthos	Puʻukaʻa	Sedge/Rush
Delissea rhytidosperma	ʻOha	Shrub
Dianella sandwicensis	ʻUkiʻuki	Herb
Dioscorea alata	Uhi	Vine
Diospyros sandwicensis	Lama	Tree
Dodonaea viscosa	ʻAʻaliʻi	Shrub
Dracena aurea	Hala pepe	Tree
Dracena auwahiensis	Hala pepe	Tree
Dracena forbesii	Hala pepe	Tree
Dracena hawaiiensis	Hala pepe	Tree
Dwarf Naupaka	Scaevola coriacea	Shrub
ʻĒkaha	Asplenium nidus	Fern
Eleocharis erythropoda	Kohekohe	Sedge/Rush
Eleocharis obtusa	Kohekohe	Sedge/Rush
Eragrostis variabilis	Kāwelu	Grass
Erythrina sandwicensis	Wiliwili	Tree

Name	Corresponding Scientific or Common Name	Plant Form as listed in Quick Reference Table
Euphorbia celastroides var. celastroides	ʻAkoko	Shrub
Euphorbia degeneri	ʻAkoko	Shrub
Fimbristylis cymosa	Mauʻu ʻakiʻaki	Sedge/Rush
Fimbristylis dichotoma	Forked fimbry	Sedge/Rush
Forked fimbry	Fimbristylis dichotoma	Sedge/Rush
Gardenia brighamii	Nāʻū	Shrub
Gossypium tomentosum	Maʻo	Shrub
Hāhā	Clermontia clermontioides	Shrub
Hala	Pandanus tectorius	Tree
Hala pepe	Dracena aurea	Tree
Hala pepe	Dracena auwahiensis	Tree
Hala pepe	Dracena forbesii	Tree
Hala pepe	Dracena hawaiiensis	Tree
Hame	Antidesma pulvinatum	Tree
Hao	Rauvolfia sandwicensis	Shrub
Hāpuʻu	Cibotium chamissoi	Fern
Hāpuʻu ʻiʻi	Cibotium menziesii	Fern
Hāpuʻu pulu	Cibotium glaucum	Fern
Hau	Hibiscus tiliaceus	Tree
Hau hele ʻula	Kokia drynarioides	Tree
Hawaiʻi sedge	Carex alligata	Sedge/Rush
Heliotropium anomalum var. argenteum	Hinahina	Shrub
Heteropogon contortus	Pili	Grass
Hibiscus arnottianus subsp. arnottianus	Kokiʻo keʻokeʻo	Shrub
Hibiscus arnottianus subsp. immaculatus	Kokiʻo keʻokeʻo	Shrub
Hibiscus arnottianus subsp. punaluuensis	Kokiʻo keʻokeʻo	Shrub
Hibiscus brackenridgei subsp. brackenridgei	Maʻo hau hele	Shrub
Hibiscus brackenridgei subsp.. mokuleianus	Maʻo hau hele	Shrub
Hibiscus brackenridgei subsp.. molokaiana	Maʻo hau hele	Shrub
Hibiscus clayi	Kokiʻo ʻula	Shrub
Hibiscus furcellatus	ʻAkiohala	Shrub
Hibiscus kokio subsp. kokio	Kokiʻo ʻula	Shrub
Hibiscus kokio subsp. Saintjohnianus	Kokiʻo ʻula	Shrub
Hibiscus tiliaceus	Hau	Tree
Hibiscus waimeae subsp. hannerae	Kokiʻo kea	Shrub
Hibiscus waimeae subsp. waimeae	Kokiʻo kea	Shrub
Hinahina	Heliotropium anomalum var. argenteum	Shrub
Hōʻawa	Pittosporum confertiflorum	Tree

Name	Corresponding Scientific or Common Name	Plant Form as listed in Quick Reference Table
Hōʻawa	*Pittosporum glabrum*	Tree
Hōʻawa	*Pittosporum hosmeri*	Tree
Hōʻawa	*Pittosporum napaliense*	Tree
Hōlei	*Ochrosia haleakalae*	Shrub
Huehue	*Coccolus orbiculatus*	Vine
Hunakai	*Ipomoea imperati*	Vine
Hydrangea arguta	Kanawao	Shrub
ʻIhi	*Portulaca lutea*	Herb
ʻIhi	*Portulaca molokiniensis*	Herb
ʻIhi	*Portulaca villosa*	Herb
ʻIhiʻihi	*Marsilea villosa*	Fern
Ilex anomala	Kāwaʻu	Tree
ʻIliahi	*Santalum freycinetianum*	Tree
ʻIliahialoʻe	*Santalum ellipticum*	Shrub
Iliau	*Wilkesia gymnoxiphium*	Shrub
ʻIlieʻe	*Plumbago zeylanica*	Herb
ʻIlima and ʻIlima papa	*Sida fallax*	Shrub
Ipomoea batatas	Uala	Vine
Ipomoea imperati	Hunakai	Vine
Ipomoea pes-caprae subsp. *brasiliensis*	Pōhuehue	Vine
Ipu	*Lageneria siceraria* and *vulgaris*	Vine
Jacquemontia sandwicensis	Pāʻū o Hiʻiaka	Vine
Kadua affinis	Manono	Tree
Kadua littoralis	Manono	Herb
Kalo	*Colocasia esculenta*	Herb
Kaluhā	*Schoenoplectiella juncoides*	Sedge/Rush
Kaluhā	*Bolboschoenus maritimus*	Sedge/Rush
Kamani	*Calophyllum inophyllum*	Tree
Kāmanomano	*Cenchrus agrimoniodes* var. *agrimoniodes*	Grass
Kanawao	*Hydrangea arguta*	Shrub
Kauila	*Alphitonia ponderosa*	Tree
Kauila	*Colubrina oppositifolia*	Tree
Kāwaʻu	*Ilex anomala*	Tree
Kāwelu	*Eragrostis variabilis*	Grass
Keahi	*Sideroxylon polynesicum*	Tree
Ki	*Cordyline fruticosa*	Shrub
Ko	*Saccharum officinarum*	Shrub
Koa	*Acacia koa*	Tree
Koaiʻa	*Acacia koaia*	Tree
Kohekohe	*Eleocharis erythropoda*	Sedge/Rush
Kohekohe	*Eleocharis obtusa*	Sedge/Rush
Kōkeʻe yellow loosestrife	*Lysimachia glutinosa*	Shrub
Kokia drynarioides	Hau hele ʻula	Tree
Kokiʻo keʻokeʻo	*Hibiscus arnottianus* subsp. *arnottianus*	Shrub

Name	Corresponding Scientific or Common Name	Plant Form as listed in Quick Reference Table
Kokiʻo keʻokeʻo	*Hibiscus arnottianus* subsp. *immaculatus*	Shrub
Kokiʻo keʻokeʻo	*Hibiscus arnottianus* subsp. *punaluuensis*	Shrub
Kokiʻo kea	*Hibiscus waimeae* subsp. *hannerae*	Shrub
Kokiʻo kea	*Hibiscus waimeae* s ubsp. *waimeae*	Shrub
Kokiʻo ʻula	*Hibiscus clayi*	Shrub
Kokiʻo ʻula	*Hibiscus kokio* subsp. *kokio*	Shrub
Kokiʻo ʻula	*Hibiscus kokio* subsp. *Saintjohnianus*	Shrub
Kōlea	*Myrsine lessertiana*	Tree
Kōlea lau liʻi	*Myrsine sandwicensis*	Shrub
Kolokolo kahakai	*Lysimachia mauritania*	Herb
Kolokolo kauhiwi	*Lysimachia hillebrandii*	Shrub
Kolokolo mokihana	*Melicope clusiifolia* (*Pelea clusiifolia*)	Shrub
Kōʻokoʻolau	*Bidens amplectans*	Herb
Kōʻokoʻolau	*Bidens hawaiensis*	Herb
Kōʻokoʻolau	*Bidens hillebrandiana*	Herb
Kōʻokoʻolau	*Bidens menziesii* subsp. *filiformis*	Shrub
Kōʻokoʻolau	*Bidens menziesii* subsp. *menziesii*	Shrub
Kōʻokoʻolau	*Bidens micrantha* subsp. *micrantha*	Herb
Kōʻokoʻolau	*Bidens torta*	Herb
Koʻoloa ʻula	*Abutilon menziesii*	Shrub
Kōpiko ʻula	*Psychotria hawaiiensis*	Tree
Kou	*Cordia subcordata*	Tree
Kūkaenēnē	*Coprosma ernodeoides*	Shrub
Kukui	*Aleurites moluccana*	Tree
Kuluʻī	*Nototrichium humile*	Shrub
Kuluʻī	*Nototrichium sandwicense*	Shrub
Kupukupu	*Nephrolepis cordifolia*	Fern
Lageneria siceraria and *vulgaris*	Ipu	Vine
Lama	*Diospyros sandwicensis*	Tree
Laukahi	*Cyclosorus hudsonianus*	Fern
Lepidium bidentatum var. *o-waihiense*	ʻĀnaunau	Herb
Leptecophylla tameia-meiae	Pūkiawe	Shrub
Lipochaeta integrifolia	Nehe	Herb
Lonomea	*Sapindus oahuensis*	Tree
Loulu	*Pritchardia beccariana*	Tree
Loulu	*Pritchardia glabrata*	Tree
Loulu	*Pritchardia hillebrandii*	Tree
Loulu	*Pritchardia maideniana* (formerly *P. affinis*)	Tree
Loulu	*Pritchardia martii*	Tree
Loulu	*Pritchardia remota*	Tree

Name	Corresponding Scientific or Common Name	Plant Form as listed in Quick Reference Table
Lycium sandwicense	ʻŌhelo kai	Shrub
Lysimachia glutinosa	Kōkeʻe yellow loosestrife	Shrub
Lysimachia hillebrandii	Kolokolo kauhiwi	Shrub
Lysimachia mauritania	Kolokolo kahakai	Herb
Machaerina angustifolia	ʻUki	Sedge/Rush
Maiʻa (banana)	*Musa acuminata*	Tree
Maiapilo	*Capparis sandwichiana*	Shrub
Maile	*Alyxia stellata*	Vine
Makaloa	*Cyperus laevigatus*	Sedge/Rush
Mamaki	*Pipturus albidus*	Shrub
Māmane	*Sophora chrysophylla*	Tree
Manele, hawaiian soap-berry	*Sapindus saponaria* var. *saponaria*	Tree
Manono	*Kadua affinis*	Tree
Manono	*Kadua littoralis*	Herb
Maʻo	*Gossypium tomentosum*	Shrub
Maʻo hau hele	*Hibiscus brackenridgei* subsp. *brackenridgei*	Shrub
Maʻo hau hele	*Hibiscus brackenridgei* subsp. *mokuleianus*	Shrub
Maʻo hau hele	*Hibiscus brackenridgei* subsp. *molokaiana*	Shrub
Maʻoliʻoli	*Schiedea globosa*	Shrub
Marsilea villosa	ʻIhiʻihi	Fern
Mauʻu ʻakiʻaki	*Fimbristylis cymosa*	Sedge/Rush
Mauʻu lāʻili	*Sisyrinchium acre*	Herb
Melicope clusiifolia (Pelea clusiifolia)	Kolokolo mokihana	Shrub
Metrosideros polymorpha var. *glaberrima*	ʻŌhiʻa lehua	Tree
Metrosideros polymorpha var. *incana*	ʻŌhiʻa lehua	Tree
Metrosideros polymorpha var. *polymorpha*	ʻŌhiʻa lehua	Tree
Meyen's sedge	*Carex meyenii*	Sedge/Rush
Mezoneuron kavaiense	Uhiuhi	Tree
Microlepia strigosa var. *strigosa*	Palapalai	Fern
Milo	*Thespesia populnea*	Tree
Moa	*Psilotum nudum*	Fern
Morinda citrifolia	Noni	Tree
Musa acuminata	Maiʻa (banana)	Tree
Myoporum sandwicense	Naio	Tree
Myoporum stellatum	Naio	Shrub
Myrsine lessertiana	Kōlea	Tree
Myrsine sandwicensis	Kōlea lau liʻi	Shrub
Naio	Myoporum stellatum	Shrub
Naio, False Sandwalwood	*Myoporum sandwicense*	Tree
Nanea	*Vigna marina*	Vine

Name	Corresponding Scientific or Common Name	Plant Form as listed in Quick Reference Table
Nanea	*Vigna o-wahuensis*	Vine
Nāʻū	*Gardenia brighamii*	Shrub
Naupaka kahakai	*Scaevola taccada*	Shrub
Naupaka kuahiwi	*Scaevola gaudichaudiana*	Shrub
Naupaka kuahiwi	*Scaevola chamissoniana*	Shrub
Naupaka kuahiwi	*Scaevola gaudichaudii*	Shrub
Naupaka, Dwarf	*Scaevola coriacea*	Shrub
Nehe	*Lipochaeta integrifolia*	Herb
Neke	*Cyclosorus interruptus*	Fern
Nene leau	*Rhus sandwicensis*	Shrub
Nephrolepis cordifolia	Kupukupu	Fern
Nestegis sandwicensis	Olopua	Tree
Niu	*Cocos nucifera*	Tree
Nohu	*Tribulus cistoides*	Herb
Noni	*Morinda citrifolia*	Tree
Nototrichium humile	Kuluʻī	Shrub
Nototrichium sandwicense	Kuluʻī	Shrub
Oʻahu sedge	*Carex wahuensis* subsp. *wahuensis*	Sedge/Rush
Ochrosia haleakalae	Hōlei	Shrub
ʻŌhā	*Clermontia kakeana*	Shrub
ʻOha	*Delissea rhytidosperma*	Shrub
ʻŌhā wai nui	*Clermontia arborescens*	Shrub
ʻOhai	*Sesbania tomentosa*	Shrub
ʻOhe	*Polyscias hawaiensis* (formerly *Tetraplasandra*)	Tree
ʻOhe (bamboo)	*Schizostachyum glaucifolium*	Shrub
Ohe makai	*Polyscias sandwicensis* (formerly *Reynoldsia*)	Tree
ʻŌhelo ʻai	*Vaccinium reticulatum*	Shrub
ʻŌhelo kai	*Lycium sandwicense*	Shrub
ʻŌhelo kau lāʻau	*Vaccinium calycinum*	Shrub
Ohiʻa ʻAi,	*Syzygium malaccense*	Tree
ʻŌhiʻa lehua	*Metrosideros polymorpha* var. *glaberrima*	Tree
ʻŌhiʻa lehua	*Metrosideros polymorpha* var. *incana*	Tree
ʻŌhiʻa lehua	*Metrosideros polymorpha* var. *polymorpha*	Tree
ʻŌlapa	*Cheriodendron trigynum*	Tree
ʻOlena	*Curcuma longa*	Herb
Olomea	*Perrottetia sandwicensis*	Tree
Olonā	*Touchardia latifolia*	Shrub
Olopua	*Nestegis sandwicensis*	Tree
Osteomeles anthyllidifolia	ʻŪlei	Shrub
Paʻiniu	*Astelia menziesiana*	Herb
Palapalai	*Microlepia strigosa* var. *strigosa*	Fern
Pamakani	*Tetramolopium lepidotum* subsp. *lepidotum*	Shrub

Name	Corresponding Scientific or Common Name	Plant Form as listed in Quick Reference Table
Pandanus tectorius	Hala	Tree
Pāpala	*Charpentiera obovata*	Tree
Pāpala	*Charpentiera ovata* var. *niuensis*	Tree
Pāpala kēpau	*Pisonia brunoniana*	Tree
Pāpala kēpau	*Pisonia umbellifera*	Tree
Pā'ū o Hi'iaka	*Jacquemontia sandwicensis*	Vine
Pawale	*Rumex skottsbergii*	Shrub
Peperomia blanda var. *floribunda*	'Ala'ala wai nui	Herb
Peperomia mauiensis	'Ala'ala wai nui	Herb
Peperomia sandwicensis	'Ala'ala wai nui	Herb
Peperomia tetraphylla	'Ala'ala wai nui	Herb
Perrottetia sandwicensis	Olomea	Tree
Phytolacca sandwicensis	Pōpolo kū mai	Shrub
Pia	*Tacca leontopetaloides*	Herb
Pili	*Heteropogon contortus*	Grass
Pilo, Hupilo	*Coprosma rhynchocarpa*	Tree
Pipturus albidus	Mamaki	Shrub
Pisonia brunoniana	See *Ceodes brunoniana*	Tree
Pisonia sandwicensis	See *Rockia sandwicensis*	Tree
Pisonia umbellifera	See *Ceodes umbellifera*	Tree
Pittosporum confertiflorum	Hō'awa	Tree
Pittosporum glabrum	Hō'awa	Tree
Pittosporum hosmeri	Hō'awa	Tree
Pittosporum napaliense	Hō'awa	Tree
Plectranthus parviflorus	'Ala'ala wai nui wahine	Herb
Plumbago zeylanica	'Ilie'e	Herb
Pōhinahina	*Vitex rotundifolia*	Shrub
Pōhuehue	*Ipomoea pes-caprae* subsp. *brasiliensis*	Vine
Pōkalakala	*Polyscias racemosa* (formerly *Munroidendron*)	Tree
Polyscias hawaiensis (formerly *Tetraplasandra*)	'Ohe	Tree
Polyscias racemosa (formerly *Munroidendron*)	Pōkalakala	Tree
Polyscias sandwicensis (formerly *Reynoldsia*)	Ohe makai	Tree
Po'olā nui	*Bidens cosmoides*	Herb
Pōpolo	*Solanum americanum*	Herb
Pōpolo	*Solanum nelsonii*	Shrub
Pōpolo	*Solanum sandwicense*	Shrub
Pōpolo kū mai	*Phytolacca sandwicensis*	Shrub
Portulaca lutea	'Ihi	Herb
Portulaca molokiniensis	'Ihi	Herb

Name	Corresponding Scientific or Common Name	Plant Form as listed in Quick Reference Table
Portulaca villosa	'Ihi	Herb
Pritchardia beccariana	Loulu	Tree
Pritchardia glabrata	Loulu	Tree
Pritchardia hillebrandii	Loulu	Tree
Pritchardia affinis (see *P. maideniana*)	Loulu	Tree
Pritchardia maideniana (formerly *P. affinis*)	Loulu	Tree
Pritchardia martii	Loulu	Tree
Pritchardia remota	Loulu	Tree
Psilotum nudum	Moa	Fern
Psychotria hawaiiensis	Kōpiko 'ula	Tree
Psydrax odorata	Alahe'e	Tree
Pua kala	*Argemone glauca*	Herb
Pūkiawe	*Leptecophylla tameiameiae*	Shrub
Pu'uka'a	*Cyperus trachysanthos*	Sedge/Rush
Rauvolfia sandwicensis	Hao	Shrub
Rhus sandwicensis	Nene leau	Shrub
Ridgetop tetramolopium	*Tetramolopium filiforme*	Shrub
Rockia sandwicensis (formerly *Pisonia sandwicensis*)	Āulu	Tree
Rubus hawaiensis	'Ākala	Shrub
Rumex skottsbergii	Pawale	Shrub
Saccharum officinarum	Ko	Shrub
Sadleria cyatheoides	'Ama'u	Fern
Sadleria pallida	'Ama'u	Fern
Santalum ellipticum	'Iliahialo'e	Shrub
Santalum freycinetianum	'Iliahi	Tree
Sapindus oahuensis	Lonomea	Tree
Sapindus saponaria var. *saponaria*	Manele, hawaiian soapberry	Tree
Scaevola chamissoniana	Naupaka kuahiwi	Shrub
Scaevola coriacea	Naupaka, Dwarf	Shrub
Scaevola gaudichaudiana	Naupaka kuahiwi	Shrub
Scaevola gaudichaudii	Naupaka kuahiwi	Shrub
Scaevola taccada	Naupaka kahakai	Shrub
Schiedea globosa	Ma'oli'oli	Shrub
Schiedea hookeri	Sprawling schiedea	Herb
Schizostachyum glaucifolium	'Ohe (bamboo)	Shrub
Schoenoplectiella juncoides	Kaluhā	Sedge/Rush
Schoenoplectus tabernaemontani	'Aka'akai	Sedge/Rush
Sesbania tomentosa	'Ohai	Shrub
Sesuvium portulacastrum	'Ākulikuli	Herb
Sida fallax	'Ilima and 'Ilima papa	Shrub

Name	Corresponding Scientific or Common Name	Plant Form as listed in Quick Reference Table
Sideroxylon polynesicum	Keahi	Tree
Sisyrinchium acre	Mauʻu lāʻili	Herb
Solanum americanum	Pōpolo	Herb
Solanum nelsonii	Pōpolo	Shrub
Solanum sandwicense	Pōpolo	Shrub
Sophora chrysophylla	Māmane	Tree
Sporobolus virginicus	ʻAkiʻaki	Grass
Sprawling schiedea	Schiedea hookeri	Herb
Syzygium malaccense	Ohiʻa ʻAi,	Tree
Tacca leontopetaloides	Pia	Herb
Tephrosia purpurea	Auhuhu	Shrub
Tetramolopium filiforme	Ridgetop tetramolopium	Shrub
Tetramolopium lepidotum subsp. *lepidotum*	Pamakani	Shrub
Thespesia populnea	Milo	Tree
Touchardia latifolia	Olonā	Shrub
Tribulus cistoides	Nohu	Herb
Uala	*Ipomoea batatas*	Vine
ʻUhaloa	*Waltheria indica*	Shrub

Name	Corresponding Scientific or Common Name	Plant Form as listed in Quick Reference Table
Uhi	*Dioscorea alata*	Vine
Uhiuhi	*Mezoneuron kavaiense*	Tree
ʻUki	*Cladium jamaicense*	Sedge/Rush
ʻUki	*Machaerina angustifolia*	Sedge/Rush
ʻUkiʻuki	*Dianella sandwicensis*	Herb
ʻŪlei	*Osteomeles anthyllidifolia*	
ʻUlu	*Artocarpus altilis*	
Vaccinium calycinum	ʻŌhelo kau lāʻau	
Vaccinium reticulatum	ʻŌhelo ʻai	
Vigna marina	Nanea	
Vigna o-wahuensis	Nanea	
Vitex rotundifolia	Pōhinahina	
Waltheria indica	ʻUhaloa	
Wikstroemia monticola	ʻĀkia	
Wikstroemia oahuensis	ʻĀkia	
Wikstroemia uva-ursi	ʻĀkia	
Wiliwili	*Erythrina sandwicensis*	
Wilkesia gymnoxiphium	Iliau	
Zingiber zerumbet	ʻAwapuhi	

TABLE 2. The table includes the 24 designs from Chapter 4: 8 climate zones and 3 landscape scenarios per zone (Lanai [L], Walkway [W], and Yard [Y]). Plants from the Quick Reference (QR) Table that are featured in a design (including a summary and photo) are indicated with an X. Plants that are suggested as an alternative in a design are indicated with a *. *Note:* only plants featured or listed as alternates in a design are shown below (not all plants in the QR Table were included in a design). While we didn't have the space to include them, this does not reflect them having less landscaping value. We hope the information provided in the Quick Reference Table will allow you to swap them in as needed to best meet your landscaping needs.

Hawaiian Name or Common Name	Scientific Name	Plant Form	Coastal Arid			Coastal Dry			Cstl. Mesic			Coastal Wet			Inland Arid			Inland Dry			Inland Mesic			Inland Wet		
		Page #	44	46	48	50	52	54	56	58	60	62	64	66	68	70	72	74	76	78	80	82	84	86	88	90
			L	W	Y	L	W	Y	L	W	Y	L	W	Y	L	W	Y	L	W	Y	L	W	Y	L	W	Y
Ae 'ae	Bacopa monnieri	Herb										X	X	*												
'Ahinahina	Achyranthes splendens var. rotundata	Shrub		X																						
'Ahu'awa	Cyperus javanicus	Sedge/ Rush											X	*												
'A'ali'i	Dodonaea viscosa	Shrub	*					X							X				*	X		*				
'Ākia	Wikstroemia oahuensis	Shrub									X															
'Ākia	Wikstroemia uva-ursi	Shrub					X	X										X				X				
'Akoko	Euphorbia celastroides var. celastroides	Shrub	X																							
'Akoko	Euphorbia degeneri	Shrub			*	X	X																			
'Ākulikuli	Sesuvium portulacastrum	Herb						X						*												
Alahe'e	Psydrax odorata	Tree					X		X		*															
'Ala'ala wai nui	Peperomia blanda var. floribunda	Herb		X														*				X		*		
'Ala'ala wai nui	Peperomia mauiensis	Herb		X																		X		*		
'Ala'ala wai nui	Peperomia sandwicensis	Herb		X																		X		*		
'Ala'ala wai nui	Peperomia tetraphylla	Herb		X																		X		*		
'Ala'ala wai nui wahine	Plectranthus parviflorus	Herb					X									X										
Alena, nena	Boerhavia repens	Herb						*									*									
Ālula	Brighamia insignis	Shrub							X												X					
'Ama'u	Sadleria cyatheoides	Fern										*													X	*
'Ama'u	Sadleria pallida	Fern																							X	*
'Awapuhi	Zingiber zerumbet	Herb								X				X										X		
'Āweoweo	Chenopodium oahuense	Shrub		*											*											
Bonamia	Bonamia menziesii	Vine																X								
Dwarf Naupaka	See Naupaka																									
Hala	Pandanus tectorius	Tree										*		X												
Hala pepe	Dracena aurea	Tree																			X	X				
Hala pepe	Dracena auwahiensis	Tree																X	X		X	X				
Hala pepe	Dracena forbesii	Tree																X	X		X	X				
Hala pepe	Dracena hawaiiensis	Tree																X	X		X	X				

Hawaiian Name or Common Name	Scientific Name	Plant Form	44	46	48	50	52	54	56	58	60	62	64	66	68	70	72	74	76	78	80	82	84	86	88	90
			Coastal Arid			Coastal Dry			Cstl. Mesic			Coastal Wet			Inland Arid			Inland Dry			Inland Mesic			Inland Wet		
			L	W	Y	L	W	Y	L	W	Y	L	W	Y	L	W	Y	L	W	Y	L	W	Y	L	W	Y
Hame	Antidesma pulvinatum	Tree								X																	
Hāpu'u	Cibotium chamissoi	Fern																							*	X
Hāpu'u 'i'i	Cibotium menziesii	Fern																							*	X
Hāpu'u pulu	Cibotium glaucum	Fern																							*	X
Hau hele 'ula	Kokia drynarioides	Tree																X								
Hawai'i sedge	Carex alligata	Sedge/Rush																							*	*
Hinahina	Heliotropium anomalum var. argenteum	Shrub			X		X																			
Hō'awa	Pittosporum confertiflorum	Tree																			X	*	X			
Hō'awa	Pittosporum glabrum	Tree																			X	*	X			
Hō'awa	Pittosporum hosmeri	Tree																			X	*	X			
Hō'awa	Pittosporum napaliense	Tree																			X					
'Ihi	Portulaca lutea	Herb	X																							
'Ihi	Portulaca molokiniensis	Herb			*																					
'Ihi	Portulaca villosa	Herb														X										
'Ihi'ihi	Marsilea villosa	Fern							X										X			X				
'Iliahialo'e	Santalum ellipticum	Shrub	X																							
'Ilie'e	Plumbago zeylanica	Herb			X											X	X	X		X						
'Ilima and 'Ilima papa	Sida fallax	Shrub			*	X			X			X			X		X					X				
Ipu	Lageneria siceraria and vulgaris	Vine												*												*
Kalo	Colocasia esculenta	Herb									X	X	X	X												X
Kaluhā	Schoenoplectiella juncoides	Sedge/Rush																							*	
Kauila	Alphitonia ponderosa	Tree																					*			
Kauila	Colubrina oppositifolia	Tree																		*						
Ki	Cordyline fruticosa	Shrub							*	X	X	X	X											X		
Ko	Saccharum officinarum	Shrub (shrub-like)								*																
Ko'oloa 'ula	Abutilon menziesii	Shrub													*	X	X									
Koa	Acacia koa	Tree																					*			
Koai'a	Acacia koaia	Tree															X									
Kohekohe	Eleocharis obtusa	Sedge/Rush																							X	
Kō'oko'olau	Bidens amplectans	Herb																	X							
Kō'oko'olau	Bidens hawaiensis	Herb																	X							
Kō'oko'olau	Bidens hillebrandiana	Herb												*												
Kō'oko'olau	Bidens menziesii subsp. filiformis	Shrub						X											X		X					

Hawaiian Name or Common Name	Scientific Name	Plant Form	Coastal Arid			Coastal Dry			Cstl. Mesic			Coastal Wet			Inland Arid			Inland Dry			Inland Mesic			Inland Wet		
Page #			44	46	48	50	52	54	56	58	60	62	64	66	68	70	72	74	76	78	80	82	84	86	88	90
			L	W	Y	L	W	Y	L	W	Y	L	W	Y	L	W	Y	L	W	Y	L	W	Y	L	W	Y
Kō'oko'olau	*Bidens menziesii* subsp. *menziesii*	Shrub						X											X		X					
Kō'oko'olau	*Bidens micrantha* subsp. *micrantha*	Herb																		X	X					
Kō'oko'olau	*Bidens torta*	Herb																		X	X					
Koki'o kea	*Hibiscus waimeae* subsp. *hannerae*	Shrub																					*		*	
Koki'o kea	*Hibiscus waimeae* subsp. *waimeae*	Shrub																					*		*	
Koki'o ke'oke'o	*Hibiscus arnottianus* subsp. *arnottianus*	Shrub																					X	X		X
Koki'o ke'oke'o	*Hibiscus arnottianus* subsp. *immaculatus*	Shrub																					X	X		X
Koki'o ke'oke'o	*Hibiscus arnottianus* subsp. *punaluuensis*	Shrub																					X	X		X
Kou	*Cordia subcordata*	Tree			*			X			*															
Kukui	*Aleurites moluccana*	Tree									*															
Kulu'ī	*Nototrichium sandwicense*	Shrub														X		X								
Kupukupu	*Nephrolepis cordifolia*	Fern																			*	*				
Lonomea	*Sapindus oahuensis*	Tree																	X							
Loulu	*Pritchardia beccariana*	Tree																							*	
Loulu	*Pritchardia glabrata*	Tree																							*	
Loulu	*Pritchardia hillebrandii*	Tree							X			X	X													
Loulu	*Pritchardia maideniana* (formerly *P. affinis*)	Tree				*			*																	
Loulu	*Pritchardia martii*	Tree																							*	
Loulu	*Pritchardia remota*	Tree				X																				
Ma'oli'oli	*Schiedea globosa*	Shrub	X			*	X																			
Ma'o	*Gossypium tomentosum*	Shrub		X	X																					
Ma'o hau hele	*Hibiscus brackenridgei* subsp. *brackenridgei*	Shrub													X		*			X						
Ma'o hau hele	*Hibiscus brackenridgei* subsp. *mokuleianus*	Shrub													X		*			X						
Ma'o hau hele	*Hibiscus brackenridgei* subsp. *molokaiana*	Shrub													X		*			X						
Mai'a (banana)	*Musa acuminata*	Tree								*																
Maiapilo	*Capparis sandwichiana*	Shrub				X		X							*		X									
Maile	*Alyxia stellata*	Vine																					X			
Mamaki	*Pipturus albidus*	Shrub																					X			

Hawaiian Name or Common Name	Scientific Name	Plant Form	Coastal Arid			Coastal Dry			Cstl. Mesic			Coastal Wet			Inland Arid			Inland Dry			Inland Mesic			Inland Wet		
Page # →			44	46	48	50	52	54	56	58	60	62	64	66	68	70	72	74	76	78	80	82	84	86	88	90
			L	W	Y	L	W	Y	L	W	Y	L	W	Y	L	W	Y	L	W	Y	L	W	Y	L	W	Y
Manele, hawaiian soapberry	*Sapindus saponaria var. saponaria*	Tree																				X				
Manono	*Kadua littoralis*	Herb							X					X												
Mau'u 'aki'aki	*Fimbristylis cymosa*	Sedge/ Rush	X	X											X	X	*									
Meyen's sedge	*Carex meyenii*	Sedge/ Rush																							X	*
Moa	*Psilotum nudum*	Fern						*																		
Nā'ū	*Gardenia brighamii*	Shrub																X	X		X					
Nanea	*Vigna marina*	Vine								*		X		*			*									
Nanea	*Vigna o-wahuensis*	Vine															*									
Naupaka kahakai	*Scaevola taccada*	Shrub	*								X			X												
Naupaka kuahiwi	*Scaevola chamissoniana*	Shrub																								X
Naupaka kuahiwi	*Scaevola gaudichaudii*	Shrub	*												X											
Naupaka, Dwarf	*Scaevola coriacea*	Shrub	*		X																					
Nehe	*Lipochaeta integrifolia*	Herb	X	X																						
Neke	*Cyclosorus interruptus*	Fern										X	X	X										X	X	*
Niu	*Cocos nucifera*	Tree											*	X												
Noni	*Morinda citrifolia*	Tree											*													
'Oha	*Delissea rhytidosperma*	Shrub																						X	X	X
'Ohai	*Sesbania tomentosa*	Shrub	*		X																					
'Ohe	*Polyscias hawaiensis (formerly Tetraplasandra)*	Tree																				X				
'Ohe (bamboo)	*Schizostachyum glaucifolium*	Shrub								*			*													
Ohe makai	*Polyscias sandwicensis (formerly Reynoldsia)*	Tree									*															
'Ōhelo kai	*Lycium sandwicense*	Shrub	X				X																			
'Ōhi'a lehua	*Metrosideros polymorpha var. glaberrima*	Tree																*			X					X
'Ōhi'a lehua	*Metrosideros polymorpha var. incana*	Tree																*			X					X
'Ōhi'a lehua	*Metrosideros polymorpha var. polymorpha*	Tree																*			X					X
O'ahu sedge	*Carex wahuensis subsp. wahuensis*	Sedge/ Rush				*		X	X	X									X							
'Olena	*Curcuma longa*	Herb								X				*										X	X	*
Pā'ū o Hi'iaka	*Jacquemontia sandwicensis*	Vine				X	X	*	X							X			X							
Palapalai	*Microlepia strigosa var. strigosa*	Fern										*									X	X	X		*	X
Pāpala kēpau	*Pisonia brunoniana*	Tree																			*					

Hawaiian Name or Common Name	Scientific Name	Plant Form	Coastal Arid 44 L	46 W	48 Y	Coastal Dry 50 L	52 W	54 Y	Cstl. Mesic 56 L	58 W	60 Y	Coastal Wet 62 L	64 W	66 Y	Inland Arid 68 L	70 W	72 Y	Inland Dry 74 L	76 W	78 Y	Inland Mesic 80 L	82 W	84 Y	Inland Wet 86 L	88 W	90 Y
Pili	*Heteropogon contortus*	Grass		X	X			X											X	X						
Pilo, Hupilo	*Coprosma rhynchocarpa*	Tree																								X
Pōhinahina	*Vitex rotundifolia*	Shrub							X						X	X				X						
Pōhuehue	*Ipomoea pes-caprae* subsp. *brasiliensis*	Vine												X												
Po'olā nui	*Bidens cosmoides*	Herb																			X					
Pōkalakala	*Polyscias racemosa (formerly Munroidendron)*	Tree				X																				
Pua kala	*Argemone glauca*	Herb														X	*	X								
Uala	*Ipomoea batatas*	Vine								*																
'Uki'uki	*Dianella sandwicensis*	Herb							X		X	X	*								X		X	X	X	*
'Ūlei	*Osteomeles anthyllidifolia*	Shrub									X										X		X			
'Ulu	*Artocarpus altilis*	Tree									X															
Wiliwili	*Erythrina sandwicensis*	Tree			X												*									

About the Authors

Hilary Parkinson, Go Native Subject Matter Consultant, Hawai'i Forest Institute (HFI)

Hilary has professional experience in restoration, invasive plant ecology, and has also published research on various horticultural and ecological topics. She developed the detailed content for the quick reference guide, and consulted with specialists to review the designs she created, both species selected and their layout. Hilary has an M.S. in Land Resources and Environmental Science from Montana State University and a B.S. in Horticulture from Boise State University.

Paul Arinaga, Go Native Project Manager, Hawai'i Forest Institute (HFI)

Paul is co-founder and project manager of the Go Native Project. Together with Travis Idol, HFI President and UH Mānoa Professor of Tropical Forestry and Agroforestry, Paul developed the original vision behind the project, as well as the concept for the Go Native Grower's Guide. Paul also develops conservation projects, conducts outreach, and raises funds for HFI. He has an MBA from London Business School and an M.A. in International Economics from The Johns Hopkins University.

Jonathan Price, Professor, Department of Geography and Environmental Science, University of Hawai'i at Hilo

Jonathan is a professor of geography at University of Hawai'i Hilo. In his research, he has utilized GIS to identify biodiversity hotspots for native bird and plant species, search for rare species, and locate appropriate areas for the restoration of threatened and endangered species. He adapted the work he did in "Mapping Plant Species Ranges in the Hawaiian Islands—Developing a Methodology and Associated GIS Layers" (Price et al 2012) to provide the zones and maps that form the foundation of this publication. He has a B.S. in Geography with a minor in Botany and a PhD in Geography, both from the University of California at Davis.

Tom Foye, Community Portal Coordinator, Hawai'i Forest Institute (HFI)

Tom has a long-time interest in native plants and is an avid gardener. He has been an advocate for providing support to community members and a way for them to connect. Tom also assisted in developing some of the content for the guide. He has extensive experience in grant writing and program administration for local government agencies and non-profit organizations, and was previously a volunteer Citizen Forester. He has a B.A. in Anthropology from the University of the Americas in Mexico City and a Master's in Public Health from the University of Hawai`i.

Made in the USA
Middletown, DE
10 November 2022

14462903R00069